Jim Wideman

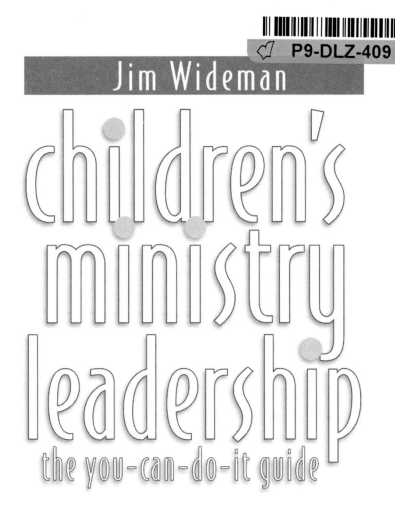

children's ministry leadership

the you-can-do-it guide

Flagship church resources

from Group Publishing

Innovations From Leading Churches

Flagship Church Resources are your shortcut to innovative and effective leadership ideas. You'll find ideas for every area of church leadership including pastoral ministry, adult ministry, youth ministry, and children's ministry.

Flagship Church Resources are created by the leaders of thriving, dynamic, and trend-setting churches around the country. These nationally recognized teaching churches host regional leadership conferences and are respected by other pastors and church leaders because their approaches to ministry are so effective. These flagship church resources reveal the proven ideas, programs, and principles that these churches have put into practice.

Flagship Church Resources currently available:

- *60 Simple Secrets Every Pastor Should Know*
- *The Perfectly Imperfect Church: Redefining the "Ideal Church"*
- *The Winning Spirit: Empowering Teenagers Through God's Grace*
- *Ultimate Skits: 20 Parables for Driving Home Your Point*
- *Doing Life With God: Real Stories Written by Students*
- *Doing Life With God 2: Real Stories Written by Students*
- *The Visual Edge: Compelling Video Connectors for Your Worship Experience*
- *Mission-Driven Worship: Helping Your Changing Church Celebrate God*
- *An Unstoppable Force: Daring to Become the Church God Had in Mind*
- *A Follower's Life: 12 Group Studies On What It Means to Walk With Jesus*
- *Leadership Essentials for Children's Ministry*
- *Keeping Your Head Above Water: Refreshing Insights for Church Leadership*
- *Seeing Beyond Church Walls: Action Plans for Touching Your Community*
- *unLearning Church: Just When You Thought You Had Leadership all Figured Out!*
- *Morph!: The Texture of Leadership for Tomorrow's Church*
- *The Quest for Christ: Discipling Today's Young Adults*
- *LeadingIdeas: To-the-Point Training for Christian Leaders*
- *Igniting Passion in Your Church: Becoming Intimate With Christ*
- *No More Lone Rangers: How to Build a Team-Centered Youth Ministry*
- *What Really Matters: 30 Devotions for Church Leadership Teams*
- *Children's Ministry Leadership: The You-Can-Do-It Guide*

With more to follow!

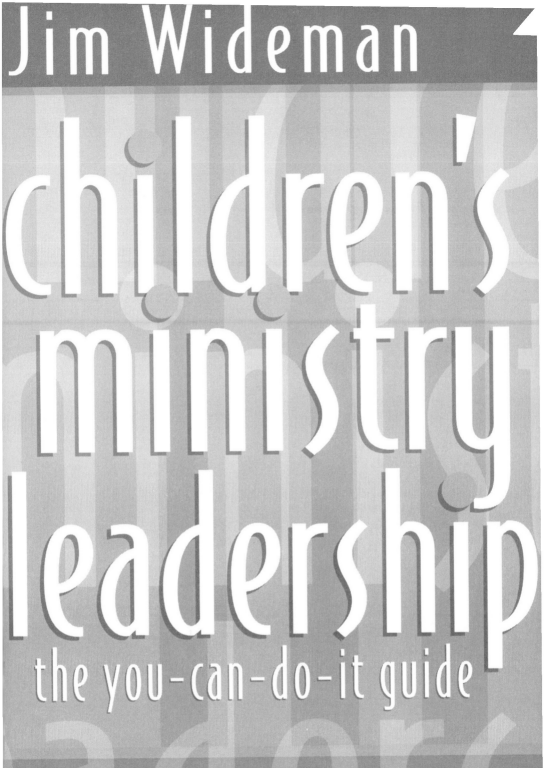

Jim Wideman

children's
ministry
leadership

the you-can-do-it guide

Children's Ministry Leadership
The You-Can-Do-It Guide

Copyright © 2003 Jim Wideman

Visit our Web site: **www.grouppublishing.com**

Credits
Editor: Jan Kershner
Chief Creative Officer: Joani Schultz
Copy Editor: Janis Sampson
Art Director: Randy Kady
Cover Art Director: Bambi Eitel
Cover Designer: toolbox creative
Print Production Artist: Tracy K. Hindman
Production Manager: Peggy Naylor

Unless otherwise noted, Scripture taken from the HOLY BIBLE, NEW INTER-
NATIONAL VERSION®. Copyright © 1973, 1978, 1984 by International Bible
Society. Used by permission of Zondervan Publishing House. All rights reserved.

LIBRARY OF CONGRESS CATALOGING-IN-PUBLICATION DATA
Wideman, Jim, 1955-
Children's ministry leadership : the you-can-do-it guide / by Jim Wideman.
    p. cm.
    ISBN 0-7644-2527-7 (pbk. : alk. paper)
    1. Church work with children. I. Title.
BV639.C4W52 2003
259'.22--dc21
                                                                  20030022
69
10 9 8 7 6 5 4 3 2 1   12 11 10 09 08 07 06 05 04 03
Printed in the United States of America.

Dedication

I'd like to dedicate this book to my fabulous family—my three girls! First, to my wonderful wife, Julie, for helping me grow and make changes to become a better leader than I ever imagined. Thanks for cleaning me up and pushing me forward. Thanks for never giving up on me and always loving me and supporting me!

And to our two girls, Yancy and Whitney. Thanks for allowing me to be a part of your worlds. You are my bright spots. Thanks for making life fun and helping me to enjoy the trip. I am proud of you and the choices you make. Thanks for allowing me the privilege to be your friend as well as your dad.

And also I would like to dedicate this book to my pastor and mentor, Pastor Willie George, and the people of Church on the Move in Tulsa, Oklahoma. I'm a better person, a better Christian, a better husband, a better dad, and a better leader because of you in my life! Thanks a million!

Contents

Introduction

You can be a leader—if you really want to be.

ENTER HERE

Some people think leadership is for a chosen few.

I couldn't disagree more.

The fact is that anyone can become a leader—if that person really *wants* to be a leader.

Think about people you know and you'll be able to name a few folks who seem to just naturally—or supernaturally—have an abundance of the stuff leadership requires. They're organized. They're focused. They're able to gather people around a cause and get things done. You look at them and think, "Those people are born leaders."

And you're half right. They have been born—but they weren't born as leaders. The skills that make them leaders are skills they've learned along the way.

We're all born into this world naked and helpless. We can't do the first thing for ourselves. There was a time you didn't know how to do anything you can now do. There was a time you couldn't dress yourself. You couldn't feed yourself. You couldn't read this book.

Now you've mastered those skills and many, many more.

You can master the skills it takes to be a leader, too. You can learn to be organized. To manage yourself and others. To be a model. They're all learned behaviors.

You see, leadership isn't about titles or paychecks or what's on your business card. You don't have to be the head of a huge ministry to be a leader. If you're influencing others, you're a leader.

But are you willing to do what it takes to be a *good* leader?

I'm a guitar player and a pretty fair one. But there are lots of guitar players who put me to shame. They're far better, and there's a reason: They've practiced more. They've done what it takes to be excellent. They've paid a price I haven't been willing to pay.

Whether you're mastering guitar chords or leading a Christian education department, it comes down to this: How bad do you want it? Are you willing to pay the price?

If the answer is yes, this book's for you. I've trained thousands of people, and I've yet to meet someone who absolutely, positively couldn't develop or sharpen leadership skills. We can all get better at leading others—guaranteed.

But there's a big condition on that guarantee: Will you do what it takes? Are you willing to make changes in your life?

When I was at college, my major was "campus-ology." That means that though I was *at* college, I wasn't really *in* college. I went to classes, but I was far more familiar with the places guitar players hung out to jam than I was familiar with the library. Being enrolled in college gave me the chance to have the time of my life.

Then Dr. Stanberry, one of my professors, pulled me aside. He said, "Jim, you've got a lot of talent and ability, but you're one of the most disorganized people I've ever met. I want to help you."

I'd seen my grade-point average. I knew I needed help. So I agreed.

Here's what he did: He bought me a calendar, the first one I'd ever owned. He showed me how to write down what I was supposed to be doing. My class schedule went into the calendar. So did my assignments. We laid it all out in black and white.

But Dr. Stanberry knew I needed more. So we regularly met and worked on using that calendar to break my disorganized habits. I had to learn to be organized.

That experience came back to me one day when I was reading 1 Corinthians 12:28. In this verse Paul lays out how we're all part of the body of Christ. We all have unique gifts and tasks, and roles to fill.

"And in the church God has appointed first of all apostles, second prophets, third teachers, then workers of miracles, also those having gifts of healing, those able to help others, those with gifts of administration, and those speaking in different kinds of tongues."

Look at the list. All these roles were appointed by the Lord. They were all sanctioned, all necessary. But look closely at the questions Paul asks in verses 29 and 30.

"Are all apostles? Are all prophets? Are all teachers? Do all work miracles? Do all have gifts of healing? Do all speak in tongues? Do all interpret?"

The obvious answer to each question is a resounding no. We're not all teachers, prophets, or healers.

I must have read that passage ten million times before I noticed that two roles Paul mentions in verse 28 aren't mentioned later. Those two roles are the ability to help others and the role of administration.

Why didn't Paul list these? I don't think it's a stretch to conclude that everyone can participate in these areas of ministry. We all can be helpers. We all can be organized and provide oversight and leadership.

Think about it: Even very young children can be helpers. Even very young Christians can be helpers. We *all* can be helpers.

And in the same way, no matter what our ministry in the church—from the senior pastor to the people directing traffic out in the parking lot—there's got to be some administration and organization in what we're doing.

Administration—one of the cornerstones of capable leadership—is for everyone. And the administrative skills that will help you provide excellent leadership can be learned, honed, and sharpened.

It takes work. It takes willingness. It isn't easy.

But the results will allow you to be more effective and fulfilled in ministry and to become the leader God knows you can be. That he designed you to be. As you add tools to your leadership toolbox, God will provide you opportunities to use those new skills to bless others and advance your ministry.

Growing in your leadership abilities is an investment—one that will pay dividends your entire life.

Ready to grow in your leadership? You *can* do it, you know!

1. Leadership From the Inside Out

If you're looking for an unlikely leader in children's ministry, I'm your guy. When I think back to how I lived in high school, even I would have voted me "least likely to succeed."

I wish I could blame someone except myself. My mother, a single mom raising two kids and supporting her own mother, did the best she could. I had a lot of friends, many of whom I'm still in touch with today. There were people in my life who cared about me. One of them, my best friend's dad, even got me a job playing guitar in a little bar band. I was making pretty good money for a kid. Of course, I was *ten* at the time and, looking back, that wasn't the smartest of decisions. One bad decision led to many bad decisions. How many? Well, to this day I don't remember my junior year in high school.

By the time the Lord got hold of me and I headed off to Bible college, I was an old, longhaired ex-dopehead, baby believer. The people at the church where I'd become a Christian hadn't dared told me to shape up; they were just glad I wasn't dealing drugs. They waited until I was heading off to school to say, "You know, maybe it would help your ministry if you quit smoking."

But when I got to Bible college, some people helped me see what I could become. Not in twenty years, but the next day. Small steps. Little steps.

And they didn't just help me remodel my outside. They helped me develop character. They focused on my inside.

You see, in the kingdom of God, leadership isn't just about getting people to follow you. Anybody can do that. All you need is force.

Maybe you've seen those old westerns where the bad guys would storm into a bank, fire a couple shots into the ceiling, and yell, "Everybody on the floor!" Those bank tellers dropped like bricks. As long as the bad guys had ammunition, they were in charge. People did what they said. But that's not a strategy I'd recommend for recruiting teachers for the fifth- and sixth-grade class.

Leadership in ministry is all about influencing others to reach the next level in their spiritual growth and their God-given skills. It's helping others develop, coaching them to become what God wants them to be.

Ministry leaders influence people. They touch the lives of others. They impact others. They don't flash their job titles around to make people fall in behind them.

True leaders—especially in ministry—grow from the inside out. Their leadership begins with their character.

Someday when you want to have fun, walk into one of those jumbo-sized chain bookstores, and ask the clerks to show you every book they have on leadership. Mercy! You'll be there all day.

Each year hundreds of books get published that describe leadership, dissect leadership, and write prescriptions for how to become a leader. Plus there are countless videos, magazines, classes, workshops, and seminars. You could spend the next six months doing nothing but studying about leadership.

At the end of that time you'd be well-informed—but not necessarily a leader. Studying leadership principles and practices like the ones you'll find in this book are just a *part* of growing as a leader. And as much as any author hates to admit it about his book, it's probably the least important part.

If you just want to get your ministry in line, you can skip on ahead a couple chapters and start doing all the things I describe. Those practical tips will get your organization oiled up and running smoothly. And you'll look more like a leader than you've ever looked.

But if you want to be a leader—an authentic leader who's got what it takes to go the distance in serving God and the people around you—then get ready for some hard, demanding work. And it starts not with your leadership techniques, but with your heart…and your willingness to respond to God's call to lead others.

That's because being a successful leader in ministry isn't measured by how many people are lined up behind you. It isn't measured by the size of your program or the number of staff working for you. It's measured by whether you're pleasing God and doing what God wants you to do.

You will see your program grow because when you listen to God and do what he says, your leadership brings increase. God blesses what you do.

That means you need to first be relying on God. Listening to God. Obeying God. And sharpening your leadership skills as you follow God where he's leading you.

The Need for Authentic Leadership

Now, I grew up in the South, and I've watched farmers work. Farmers find out right quick that just because you put seeds in the ground that doesn't mean plants will grow.

If farmers want to see a harvest, they've got to tend to the seeds, making sure there's enough water, warmth, and fertilizer. Someone's got to nurture the young plants along if down the road anyone expects to pick crops.

And just like growth on a farm can't happen without a farmer, growth in the church can't happen without a leader. You won't see growth in your Sunday school, children's church, midweek program, or anywhere else until someone says, "I'll be in charge of this, and do the things necessary to bring growth."

Leadership causes increase—and when I look in the Bible I see that it's God's will that growth happens in ministry. Jesus came to seek and to save those who are lost. We've been sent out to find those folks and bring them into the church. The church is supposed to keep getting bigger.

I get criticized now and then about being so concerned about tracking the numbers at my church. I know how many people come each week. I know how effectively we're reaching each age group. I know how much our budget is growing. I keep the numbers in front of me. Some people complain, "All you care about are nickels and noses. You live in the book of Numbers and you should live in the book of Acts."

Well, here's something I've learned: *It takes nickels to reach noses.* If your budget doesn't grow, there will be ministry opportunities you can't pursue. If your Sunday school classes don't get more crowded, there are kids you aren't reaching.

And don't confuse population shift with growth. When someone comes from another church to your church, that's not growth. That's population shift. Growth is addition. It means new kids. New families. Not kids and families that wandered in from the church down the street.

Growth—real growth—is important.

Don't get me wrong: Having a small ministry isn't a bad thing. But if a ministry stays small, that can be a sign that something is wrong. And what's wrong is often a lack of good leadership. As a rule, good leadership causes increase. Negative leadership causes stagnation.

Throughout this book I'll share techniques with you that I've picked up from the best ministry professionals I know. I'll tell you how I go about leading in my children's ministry at Church on the Move. As I write, I have seven paid staff and right at one thousand volunteer leaders serving upwards of thirty-five hundred kids each week...but I'm looking to grow. I'm always looking to grow.

Begin at the Beginning

So get ready to receive some solid advice. But not yet. First, let's talk about you.

People go into leadership positions for all sorts of reasons, sometimes for the wrong ones. I suspect if you're reading this book you're in a children's ministry leadership position. But are you a leader?

We can't forsake our first love—God—because we get distracted by doing ministry.

There's an easy way to find out the answer to that question. Look over your shoulder. Is anyone back there following you? If not, you're not leading—you're just marching in a very short parade.

If you *are* leading others, whether it's one or one thousand, you've got to decide whether you're willing to do it God's way. If so, you've got to be willing to be a servant in three important ways:

BE A SERVANT OF GOD.

I don't know about you, but I want to hear, "Well done, good and faithful servant" one day. God doesn't hand out that welcome just because you've got "Children's Pastor" on your business card.

God reserves his praise for those who love him…follow him…and serve him. What's important to God is our hearts. We church leaders can't get so swelled up with self-importance that we forget to answer, "Yes, Lord" when God asks us to do something. We can't forsake our first love—God—because we get distracted by doing ministry.

Do people around you compliment you on how much you get accomplished—or on how much your character reflects the character of God? Are you trusting, following, and serving God?

BE A SERVANT OF OTHERS.

If you signed up so you could run the show or because you want to show people how a good program is supposed to be run, you're in for a rude awakening.

God just doesn't honor puffed-up leaders. He's funny that way—he isn't impressed with us. Maybe that's because if his Son died on a cross to serve and save us, God figures we ought to be good for moving a few tables or listening to someone who's upset.

Do people around you describe you as a servant? Why or why not?

BE A SERVANT OF THE TRUTH.

If you're going to lead in ministry, you need a clear understanding of God's Word. What's the point of putting together a powerhouse organization if you don't have a purpose? if you're not fulfilling *God's* purposes for your ministry?

Is your heart in tune with God's heart for your ministry? Are you praying? growing in your relationship with God? digging into his Word?

You can't lead people someplace you've never been. If you want your ministry to grow deeper in the things of the Lord, go there yourself. Seek after God, and then invite others to follow along with you on the journey.

Ministry leadership—authentic ministry leadership—doesn't demand that we be perfect. But it does demand that we be people after God's heart…from the inside out. And God is perfectly happy to give us the challenges we need to develop leadership character.

Think about Moses. Now, I've never met the man, but I've thought a lot about him. I think if we had met Moses when he was still living in Pharaoh's household, we'd have recruited him onto our church board in a heartbeat. I suspect he looked and sounded like a leader—educated and trained in the court of a mighty king. He probably wore fine clothes and the confident look of a man who was used to being taken seriously.

But he wasn't a leader fit for God's people. Not yet.

God had built all the right stuff into Moses. God knew he was going to call Moses into leadership. But I think before Moses could be used, he had to go tend sheep out in the wilderness with Jethro. Moses needed to grow in his understanding of his people's history and culture. Moses needed to learn to rely on God.

God didn't have Moses herd sheep for forty years to punish Moses. God used those years to prepare Moses for leadership, to season and shape him.

Like Moses, before we get too busy *doing* leadership, we've got to learn to follow God and let God shape us into leaders. Authentic leaders, from the inside out.

You ready for the ride?

Let's go!

2. Seven Traits of Authentic Leadership

Leadership is a double-edged sword: Leaders can use their influence for good—or evil. Churches have leaders, but so do gangs. Martin Luther was a leader, but so was Adolph Hitler.

Leadership skills aren't good or bad; it all depends how you use them. Luther organized a religious movement and Hitler a holocaust. Same skills.

Please understand that when I talk about being a leader I mean being a *Christian* leader. A leader serving in ministry. If that's your calling, you'll find there are things required of you that aren't required if you're leading a company, a revolution, or a rock band.

I'd like to suggest that there are seven things you need to *be* if you want to exert authentic leadership in ministry. (I'll get to the list of things you need to *do* in the next chapter.)

1. You've got to be willing to change.

Let me ask the same question I asked in the introduction: How bad do you want to be a leader? Are you willing to pay the price?

The price tag includes changing how you do things. Trying new things. Drop-kicking what you're doing now out of the way so you can start over. Are you willing to change how you think about yourself and your ministry? Are you willing to honestly admit your strengths and weaknesses?

During my twelve years at Church on the Move, I've grown more in my leadership skills than in my entire past ministry. Why? Because I now desire to grow in my abilities and depth as a leader. Now I'm willing to make changes.

Are you willing to grow?

2. You've got to have integrity.

Integrity is uprightness of character. Lining up with God's Word. Being the same inside as you are outside—transparent through and through.

To lead in ministry you don't have to be right all the time—which is a relief for me because I flunked the perfection test a long time ago. But you do need to give up the desire to have people *think* you're always right.

Admit it: You like having people think you're right. It's just human, especially for leaders. We think it builds confidence in the troops when they see us make decisions and stand firm.

Except we aren't always right. We're wrong a lot. And nobody admires leaders who are too proud or scared to admit they don't know it all. Remember: It's not about your being right; it's about God being right and you leading the way to him.

3. You've got to be faithful in small things.

Faithful people handle small things well. They work with the resources they have, and they're careful stewards of those resources.

If I've heard it once, I've heard it a hundred times: "I just can't tell kids about Jesus with a budget so small. If I had more money, I'd be effective."

My answer is this: "No you wouldn't. If you're not being faithful to serve kids with the budget you've got, you don't deserve more. How you handle little things is exactly how you'll handle big things."

That principle holds for us leaders, too. If you want to grow in your sphere of influence and responsibility, first do excellent work in handling the tasks at hand. Then you'll be rewarded with more.

When people join our volunteer staff at Church on the Move, they don't start at the top. First, we want to see if they're faithful handling the small stuff. Jesus lays out the principle in Luke 16:10: "Whoever can be trusted with very little can also be trusted with much, and whoever is dishonest with very little will also be dishonest with much."

We want faithful people on staff. They're committed to God's Word, and that ultimately brings them success in ministry. They're committed to others, consistently serving the people God has placed around them.

Faithful people get where God wants them and they stay there, no matter what. They plug in and stay plugged in. They're dependable.

Would the people who know you best say you're faithful? Why or why not?

4. You must be a person of vision— and communicate that vision.

Proverbs 29:18 says, "Where there is no revelation [vision], the people cast off restraint; but blessed is he who keeps the law." This highlights pretty clearly what happens when there's no vision in a person's life.

Having a great vision for your ministry is wonderful, but not as wonderful as when a great vision has hold of *you*. If, after prayer, you know in your bones that God wants your ministry to include kids from a neighborhood no other church is serving, the challenge of finding a bus and a driver won't slow you down. You'll overcome any obstacle—because you know for certain what God wants you to do. A great ministry vision is clear, big, and captures your energy and imagination.

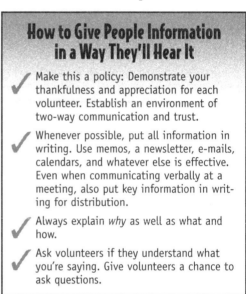

How to Give People Information in a Way They'll Hear It

✓ Make this a policy: Demonstrate your thankfulness and appreciation for each volunteer. Establish an environment of two-way communication and trust.

✓ Whenever possible, put all information in writing. Use memos, a newsletter, e-mails, calendars, and whatever else is effective. Even when communicating verbally at a meeting, also put key information in writing for distribution.

✓ Always explain *why* as well as what and how.

✓ Ask volunteers if they understand what you're saying. Give volunteers a chance to ask questions.

And when a great vision has hold of you, sharing your vision will draw others who share your vision. They'll line up to be on your team. They'll stick, because they care about what you care about.

What stops us in our ministries usually isn't a lack of people, it's a lack of people who share our vision. No wonder people don't respond when we ask for their help—we haven't cast our vision out there in a compelling fashion.

Here's how that played out in my life. At my first church I had a children's church of seven kids: six well-behaved kids and Little Bubba.

I'd come home every Sunday and tell my wife, Julie, everything that had gone wrong that morning. Little Bubba had grabbed Sally and slammed her up against the wall. Little Bubba had gone after Billy. I'd had to pick up after Little Bubba until I was about half-crazy.

Then I'd ask Julie for her help in children's church. Julie would remind me once again that she wasn't remotely interested in helping me, thank you very much.

So I complained to the Lord about it. "Lord, this woman you gave me won't help me in children's church. What's up with that? Can't you soften her heart or something?"

Well, the Lord asked me to listen to what I was saying to her. To listen to the words coming out of my mouth when I talked about children's ministry.

I hadn't mentioned Kevin worshipping God in children's church or how Mary loved Jesus and prayed for her friends. I hadn't told Julie about the great things God was doing. I was too busy describing how Little Bubba was terrorizing the class.

I even made Little Bubba jokes:

Q: What's the best way to tell how bad Little Bubba's behavior will be this week?

A: See if there's a full moon.

What do your words and attitude communicate?

I thought that stuff was *funny*. So my wife, based on what I said to her, thought children's church was a roomful of Little Bubbas ready to take her hostage.

I knew what that children's ministry could become. I knew where God could take it for his glory. But I certainly wasn't communicating that vision to my wife. When I stopped to listen to what I'd been telling Julie, I wouldn't have wanted to work with me either.

So I changed how I talked. I shared the good things that happened, and within a few days Julie asked me a question.

"Does Little Bubba still go to our church?"

I said, "Yes, but last Sunday during praise time he raised one hand halfway. I believe revival has hit Little Bubba."

And she said, "You know, I think I'll stop by and help out."

In one moment I doubled my workforce, and Julie and I got on the same team. That was a great moment—and it would never have happened if I hadn't started speaking the vision.

How do you describe to the people around you what you're doing? What do your words and attitude communicate? Are you willing to lay aside complaining and cynicism and be relentlessly positive?

5. You've got to be willing to follow others.

Good leaders are also good followers. They submit to the authority God has placed in their lives.

I believe children's pastors work for the senior pastors in their churches. If your pastor's vision for your church is to enter into a time of deepening discipleship, your children's programming should reflect and reinforce that purpose. If evangelism is the new focus, embrace that.

When we follow the leaders God has placed in our lives, we benefit from their wisdom and experience.

Think about a lowly private who's huddled in a foxhole while his squad is under enemy fire. He knows someone out there is shooting his direction, and he knows if he keeps his head down he's safe for the moment.

Then he hears his lieutenant shout out, "Everybody up! We're moving forward!"

Those are not words privates under fire like to hear.

But what the private doesn't know is that his lieutenant was on the radio with headquarters. And headquarters knows from surveillance and reconnaissance that the enemy line is weakest straight ahead. *That's* the direction to go if the private wants to survive.

By following his leader and charging forward, the private benefits from information he couldn't get from the bottom of a foxhole.

Your pastor may well have more information than you have about where the Lord is taking your church. So if you're leading your children's ministry without being under your pastor's authority and leadership, you're in trouble.

In what ways are you following as you lead?

6. You've got to be unpopular at times.

Paul knew his young friend Timothy was going to be dealing with church people, so he wrote this to Timothy: "You then, my son, be strong in the grace that is in Christ Jesus" (2 Timothy 2:1).

Leaders aren't always popular. Paul didn't advise Timothy to express leadership by pushing people around, demanding his own way, or manipulating people. The strength Timothy needed was to be strong in grace as he dealt with others and himself.

Leaders need that kind of strength because it's true: It *is* lonely at the top.

As a leader you'll sometimes have to stand alone, drawing lines not everyone is willing to cross. Leaders aren't always popular.

I've watched the Miss America pageant once or twice, and I've noticed the young lady who wins the Miss America tiara seldom wins the Miss Congeniality award. Apparently, doing what it takes to win the tiara doesn't necessarily make a candidate popular. That's true for leadership too. Few effective, strong leaders will end up in the running for Miss Congeniality.

Now, I care about people and I want them to like me, but here's the truth: It really doesn't matter if they do.

Read through the Gospels, and you'll see that Jesus didn't worry all that much about popularity either. Calling the local religious leaders a "brood of vipers" wasn't a move calculated to win friends.

Jesus called things the way he saw them. As a leader you have to do the same thing, and that can be a quick ticket to Loneliness Junction.

Are you willing to make the unpopular calls? To stand alone when following God's leading requires it?

7. You've got to be someone people see as a leader.

If you want others to think of you as a leader, look like one. Carry yourself like one. Respond and react like one. Use your time the way leaders use their time—effectively. Handle criticism the way leaders handle it—by learning from it.

Put the principles and recommendations you find in this book into practice, and do it in full view of your volunteers and staff. The first time you show up in the back of a teacher's class with a clipboard and evaluation form (see page 24), you'll communicate loud and clear that you're leading.

People haven't got any choice but to love you—the Bible tells them they're required to do that. But you've got to earn their respect.

Are you willing to do what it takes to help others see you as a leader? What's holding you back?

Leader Observation Checklist

Date: _____ Leader observed: _____

Classroom or ministry area observed: _____

1. Is there a bottleneck in the registration or pick-up process?

☐ Yes   ☐ No

Comments:

2. Does the classroom look organized and is the lesson flowing well?

☐ Yes   ☐ No

Comments:

3. Is the classroom well-staffed?

☐ Yes   ☐ No

Comments:

4. Do workers lead with ease and confidence?

☐ Yes   ☐ No

Comments:

5. Are the kids enjoying the class?

☐ Yes   ☐ No

Comments:

6. What are the workers doing right?

7. Where do you see room for improvement?

3. Ten Leadership Fundamentals

Authentic leadership is more than the potential to lead. It's even more than proven character in someone called by God to a leadership position. Authentic leadership is expressed in action, too. It's one thing to talk leadership and quite another to demonstrate it.

Here are ten fundamentals you'll need to master—fundamentals we'll walk through together in more detail later in this book.

For now, let's take a quick overview and see how you're doing.

1. Leaders set an example in their personal lives.

If you want people to follow you, give them something worth following.

As a leader, how you live your life is far more important than where your name appears on an organizational chart. How you treat your spouse, how you treat your children, how you honor God.

The highest compliment I was ever paid came when a man at church walked up to me after church one Sunday. He said, "I've been watching how you get along with your teenagers. Man, I want to take lessons from you. That's what I want with my four-year-old when he gets to be that age."

I about started crying. Here was a man who believed that my relationship with my family was worth following. He saw us as an example.

How you follow your pastor sets an example, too. I would love for everyone who serves in my children's ministry to treat me the way I treat my pastor. I set the example.

When my pastor calls a meeting, I'm not late. When my pastor wants to see me, I drop everything and get there. I don't check call-waiting calls when I'm talking with my pastor. My pastor is an authority in my life, and I communicate my respect.

When it comes to leadership, the golden rule applies big time: You need to treat people in the way you want to be treated. How you treat your leaders and how you treat those you lead—it all matters. You're an example.

2. Leaders are problem solvers.

Leaders aren't derailed by problems. They meet challenges with a spirit of faith in God's ability to overcome those challenges.

I know it's popular to say that there are no such things as "problems," just "opportunities." Well, I'm here to tell you: Now and then Brother Jim has *problems.*

When there aren't enough drivers for a field trip, that's a problem. When there's not enough budget to cover the growth you're experiencing, that's a problem. When a pipe breaks and floods the preschool room, that's a problem.

And if you're the leader, people will expect you to solve those problems.

Leaders aren't afraid to get their hands dirty. They see that problems get solved—period. They identify the problems and get them fixed. We'll take a look at a strategy for whipping problems into shape in Chapter 10.

3. Leaders show initiative.

Leaders don't wait to be told what to do or shrink from challenges. They don't hide in their offices hoping things get better when the bottom drops out of a program or a chance to improve presents itself. They're proactive.

I'm a big believer in the "Santa" approach to making things happen around our church. As I walk around on Sunday morning, I make a list— and then I check it twice. (For a sample checklist, look at page 24.)

I may jot down that a particular greeter did a great job helping children feel welcome or that a teacher needs more training in how to present a Bible lesson. During the following week, I'll write a note to the greeter and see that the teacher gets some coaching.

Then the next Sunday, I'll check to see that the greeter is still greeting and the teacher has improved. And as I go, I'm working on another list. I've always got a list of things to affirm and things to improve.

I've discovered that what I expect may or may not happen. But what I inspect gets done. So I inspect often. Do the same—show initiative in fixing problems, shoring up weak spots, and celebrating strong performance.

4. Leaders manage their time well.

We'll talk more about time management in Chapter 6 because if you can't manage your time, you'll be stuck reacting to people and situations. You'll never be effective. You'll never be a strong leader.

But with time management, you'll amaze even yourself.

Let me say right here that managing your time isn't just about getting lots of stuff done. It's about getting the *right* things done...the *best* things done...and that means doing what God wants you to do.

5. Leaders patiently demonstrate how they want things done.

Effective leaders strike a balance between showing and telling.

If all you ever do is tell people how to do ministry, they'll soon grow frustrated. They need to see it in action to really understand. But if you do all the work yourself and never explain what you're doing, they'll also fail to learn. You've got to both show and tell. Demonstrate and explain.

You'll know you've found the right balance when your workers can describe what you want because you've told them and they've seen you do it.

6. Leaders invest in others through coaching.

Leaders come alongside people and help them get better at what they do. They become coaches.

A good coach starts with what a player can already do and builds on it. No football coach spends time teaching a quarterback how to tackle. That's not the quarterback's job. Of course, there are fundamentals everyone needs to know—the rules, how to catch, how to throw. But that's about it.

A wise football coach doesn't want each player to be equally good at every position. A wise football coach wants to make each player outstanding at whatever position that player fills.

What do your individual volunteers do well? Do you know? What's your individualized development plan for each volunteer in your ministry?

If you don't have one, sharpen your pencil. You've got some work to do. Write a development plan for each of the people who report directly to you in your ministry. Is it easy? No—but good coaching never is.

7. Leaders take appropriate risks.

Now and then it pays to be ignorant. I'm living proof.

During my first few years in children's ministry, back in the '70s, my church didn't have the money to send me to conferences. I'm glad because if I'd gone I would have been told that what I wanted to do was impossible.

You see, we had seven kids in our ministry. We wanted more kids. And we wanted kids to understand how they fit into our church.

I asked the Lord what we should do, and it seemed clear we were supposed to involve our kids in helps ministries. So down in children's church we plugged kids in as deacons and got kids involved in service. Pretty soon we had more than three hundred kids, and I was invited to speak at those conferences I hadn't attended.

I'm so glad I listened to the Lord instead of "thus sayeth the seminar speaker."

So I showed up, made my little presentation, and there were lots of confused faces. It turned out that what we'd done wasn't supposed to work. It couldn't work—and people lined up to let me know it. Kids couldn't possibly do ministry—they'd never follow through, the whole model was sure to fail.

But when I got home, there it was. Working.

I'm so glad I listened to the Lord instead of "thus sayeth the seminar speaker." Had we taken risks to try something new? Since we were following God's direction, there was no risk at all.

But even if we'd moved ahead without a clear word from God, the only risk we'd taken was involving children in ministry. We'd risked a little bit of money, a lot of time, and my reputation. So what if we'd failed? We would have done something else to reach and disciple those kids.

What risks are you taking in your ministry?

8. Leaders bear fruit and grow spiritually.

Leaders carry more responsibility than followers and face greater challenges. They handle extra stress, extra work, and often make do with fewer resources than they wish they had. Those aren't ideal conditions for growth.

Yet even in difficult situations leaders grow. They don't focus on what they're lacking—they focus on who they follow. And their faithfulness bears fruit in their lives.

How do you see yourself growing in your relationship with God? Are you deepening your commitment? growing in love?

9. Leaders don't worry about comparisons.

People aren't in the church long before they realize that leaders come and go. And it seems you're always following a leader that people liked better than you.

Don't worry about comparisons. You can't talk your way out of them by pointing out the shortcomings of the person who was on staff before you. You have to do something that helps folks see you for who *you* are.

But even that's not enough sometimes.

There are plenty of times I've come along behind someone else and looked pretty pale by comparison. But let me tell you about one of those rare times I was actually the guy who was used as a yardstick of excellence.

While I was on staff at a church, my team and I had been particularly successful in launching some programs. I'd moved on, but once when I was back in town I stopped by the church to see how things were going.

The children's pastor was gracious and invited me into his office. He shook his head and said, "If I hear one more 'Brother Jim story' I'm going to throw up." He'd had way too many people tell him how it used to be and how Brother Jim had done this or that.

I told the children's pastor the solution was simple: Do something that worked for him that Brother Jim wouldn't have done. Something that Brother Jim *couldn't* do. There were plenty of ministry programs I'd never been able to get up and running.

That's when the woman who ran the church's daycare center burst into the office. She said there was a crazy guy with a rifle out in the parking lot—and he was heading toward the preschool center's playground!

The children's pastor did the right thing: He picked up the phone and called the police.

I did the stupid thing: I ran outside to see what I could do. I got to the parking lot and sure enough—the daycare workers were quickly herding kids inside where they'd be safe. But the man with a rifle was already there.

I parked myself between the kids and the man, who was obviously disturbed. I said as sternly as I could, "Gimme that gun!"

He tossed it to me.

So I pointed and shouted, "Now get out of here!" He ran off.

No sooner was he out of sight when the police arrived. They were looking for a crazed-looking man holding a gun, and sure enough, there I was. I fit the description *exactly*.

Once we straightened out why they shouldn't shoot me, the police sped off to look for the real trespasser while my knees shook at the thought of what I'd done. It turned out the man had escaped from a mental hospital, broken into a house, taken a gun, and was headed toward the playground for no apparent reason.

The children's pastor couldn't believe it. Just when he was about to come out from under my shadow, I'd shown up, faced down a gunman, and maybe saved a bunch of preschoolers. His life wasn't going to get easier anytime soon.

I don't share this story to show how big or strong I am. I was an idiot, pure and simple, and it's God's grace that it worked out all right. I share this story because even with all that working against him, in time, that children's pastor established his own effective programs and put the Brother Jim stories behind him.

And if someone can get past that, you can establish your leadership where you are. Give it some time, take action, and let God work through you.

With whom are you comparing yourself? What's the result? What if you could just put the comparisons aside?

10. Leaders are lifelong learners.

Lots of professions require continuing education units. If you're a doctor or a nurse and you quit learning, sooner or later your license to practice medicine will be taken away from you.

I wish we had something like that in children's ministry.

Working with a mentor is worth its weight in gold.

Children's ministry, as a field, has way too many know-it-alls. People who hit on a successful idea and never grow past it.

The fact is you don't know it all. I know I don't. And the people we lead in our children's ministries are *certain* we don't. We've all got things to learn, and if you're not leading the way in learning, you can't expect the people you direct to keep learning and growing either.

I don't mean you need to get another degree. The place to start is to find a mentor—someone who's wiser and more experienced than you—and go ask questions. Then listen to the answers and the questions that come back at you.

Working with a mentor is worth its weight in gold. You'll not only learn something, but you'll become teachable. And that's right where you need to stay.

Read books. Listen to tapes. Go to workshops and conferences. And be sure you tell your volunteers what you're learning. Your example says it's OK to admit you don't know it all. And it's OK to go find out what you need to know.

My mother taught me this: Experience is the best teacher—but it doesn't have to be *your* experience.

I visit other churches and learn from them. There's not a big church in my area where I haven't nosed around to discover what they're doing and why.

If a church near you spent three months preparing a program that looked great on paper but failed miserably with the kids in your community, wouldn't you want to know about that? I would. I want to learn from the experiences of others. That's a continuing education credit where someone else paid the tuition.

Leaders are lifelong learners. What have you learned lately?

4. Thinking Like a Leader

PILOT CAR
FOLLOW ME

Authentic leadership begins with what you are and is then expressed in what you do. And somewhere along the way it changes how you think, too.

You quit thinking like a follower. You begin thinking like a leader.

Thinking like a leader isn't just about having more information than the next person. Having information doesn't make you a leader. It makes you an encyclopedia.

Moses was a man who had plenty of information. He'd been raised by the Egyptians, who were at the top of their game when Moses came along.

And Moses was raised not only by the Egyptians, he was raised by Egyptian royalty.

Moses was exposed to the best of everything—science, art, and culture. The Egyptians got the religion part wrong, but when it came to leadership training and problem solving, they had it nailed. Those pyramids didn't build themselves.

At the palace, Moses was trained to run the country. He was trained daily for leadership on a national scale. And sadly, that's not something Moses would have learned if God had left him in the Israelite culture.

The Israelites had a slave mentality. A follower mentality. For hundreds of years they'd practiced waiting for something to happen that would rescue them from slavery. While they get high marks for faithfulness, they weren't especially effective leaders. They weren't making anything happen.

So God plucked Moses out of the Israelites' culture and slave mentality and had him raised by Egyptians. God made a way for Moses' real mother to be there to teach him about the things of God, so Moses got the best of both worlds: an Egyptian education and religious training at the knee of his mother.

And even all that didn't adequately prepare and season Moses for the amazing leadership role God later gave him.

When God called Moses to a ministry, Moses still had some things to learn about leadership. He still made mistakes. And if you're called into ministry, you'll have some things to learn about leadership as you go, too. Starting with how you think about leadership and your place as a leader.

In Exodus 3:11, we get an idea of how Moses viewed himself as a leader. God had just given him a very clear assignment: Go bring God's people out of Egypt. Moses replies, "Who am I, that I should go to Pharaoh and bring the Israelites out of Egypt?"

Moses wasn't thinking like a leader. He wasn't even thinking like a follower. He offered excuses and questioned God's choice of messengers. Moses didn't want anything to do with the entire enterprise.

What had happened to the confidence Moses had as an adopted grandson of Pharaoh? It was gone. What had happened to Moses' willingness to obey God and do as he was told? It was nowhere in sight. Even when God supplied him with a plan, a helper, and a couple miracles to pull out as proof that Moses represented God, Moses shied away from the assignment.

Moses wasn't thinking like a leader—yet!

And maybe you're not thinking like a leader either.

Now, if you're reading this book, you're probably in a leadership position. God's entrusted some tasks or some people to your care. And you may be doing tremendous work—but are you thinking like a leader?

Leadership changes how you think about yourself.

Maybe you grew up timid, or you grew up like me—jumping into things headfirst without thinking. That's not leadership, by the way, it's recklessness. I'm lucky I lived through my childhood. God bless my mother; I think raising me ought to get her a special medal.

Leaders accept that they may have something to say when people are wandering around looking for direction. They share their ideas. They get involved in solving problems. They take responsibility.

Leadership changes how you think about others.

When you think like a leader you see that in many situations people want leadership to be expressed. It's not an intrusion. It's not arrogance. It's helpful.

Jesus called us all sheep in need of a shepherd. Hang around a church awhile, and you'll realize that people need considerable shepherding. Jesus is the good shepherd who can bring salvation, but we can be pretty good shepherds who bring order and structure. That's worth something too.

Leadership changes how you think about your own leaders.

It's easy to question decisions made by your pastor or other leaders when you've got the benefit of hindsight. Making great decisions is easy when you have the luxury of thinking about situations as long as you want.

But when you start thinking like a leader, you begin appreciating people who lead you. Authentic leaders quickly become better followers.

How we think about ourselves and our situation has a huge impact on our ability to lead. For God to use Moses as a leader, God had to help Moses overcome his slave mentality. In the church today, there are four other kinds of faulty thinking I've seen sabotage a leader's effectiveness in ministry. Do any of these sound familiar?

FAULTY THOUGHT 1: "WE'VE ALWAYS DONE IT THIS WAY."

OK, you've never actually said those words aloud. But do you act like you believe them?

Why do you arrange your Sunday school classrooms by age or gender? meet only on Sunday morning? stick with programs that quit reaching your kids ten years ago? Is it because you've always done it that way?

I'm not suggesting we question the content of what we believe and teach. But when it comes to how we deliver that content, let's not let tradition stand in our way. Traditions can cost way more than they're worth.

I once served at a church that owned an organ donated by the family of a man who'd died years before. The organ hadn't worked in years, and it sat right down front in the chapel where we did children's ministry. And I mean right down front—it squatted on prime real estate and was always in the way.

I'm a musician. Nonworking keyboards don't do much for me. I asked about fixing it and found out that parts were either unavailable or too expensive. There was no way we were ever going to get that organ working.

I asked if I could move the organ and was told there was no possible way. It had been donated by a church member. It was a memorial. It had been there for years.

I asked if I could take a picture of the organ and put it next to a picture of the dead guy on a plaque. I could nail the plaque on a wall where nobody would trip over it. Wouldn't that work as a memorial too?

The board chewed on the idea awhile and decided that maybe, if I asked the surviving family members nicely and got their permission, something could be worked out. Perhaps.

I never got that organ moved. The last I heard the final surviving kin of the dead guy had joined him in the hereafter, so maybe the organ is gone now. But maybe not—there was a lot of tradition operating there.

What traditions are hampering effective ministry in your children's ministry? They won't be as obvious as an electronic organ, so you'll need to give the question some thought. And it's possible that maybe you're the one perpetuating traditions that are slowing down your ministry.

FAULTY THOUGHT 2: "WELL, IT WORKED FOR ME."

Why do we assume the way we learned about God is the best way for everyone to learn?

There's a little church out West where a woman has taught the two- and three-year-olds Sunday school class for more than forty years. She even had the *pastor* in her class when he was that age.

Each week she gathers the children around a table, pulls out her flannel graph, and marches cutout Bible characters around the board as she tells stories. That's how she was taught, and she's not interested in doing Christian education any other way.

> **Effective leaders are open to trying new approaches and new technology.**

The children aren't allowed to touch the characters—kids literally have to *sit on their hands* during the Bible story so nobody's tempted to grab a sheep or apostle and play with it.

This woman's heart is in the right place, but her thinking is faulty. She's assuming everyone is wired just like her, everyone learns the same way she learns. Because of that, she spends half her teaching time telling kids to sit still and stay quiet.

Effective leaders are open to trying new approaches and new technology. They champion change if it helps accomplish the mission.

Are you able to lead others when it requires you to change? to try things that aren't comfortable?

FAULTY THOUGHT 3: "DON'T INTERRUPT ME; I'M BUSY LEADING."

I've got a policy at my church: Brother Jim doesn't like surprises. I mean, I *seriously* don't like them. If you're on my staff and something happens in your area of ministry, I should know about; it's your job to tell me—fast.

I don't want to be walking down the hall and get blindsided by an angry parent, angry teacher, or angry anything else. And I don't want a problem to fester because nobody brought it to my attention.

I'll take the bad news along with the good. I can't think of one time that bad news went away because I ignored it. For leaders, ignorance is not bliss.

If you're going to lead, you've got to stay open and approachable. Do those words describe you?

Here's a test: Ask ministry peers how well you listen. How easy is it to give you bad news? What do they say?

It's especially important you make it very, very easy for people to give you bad news. Otherwise you'll hear only the good stuff, and that's usually only part of the story.

How to Get People to Tell You Bad News

1. Don't shoot the messengers. If you explode at the person who calls you Saturday night to report the children's ministry's sound system won't work, that's the last time anyone gives you a heads-up warning. You need to *thank* people who bring you bad news. Not the people who caused the bad news, but those who reported it. They're your early alert system.

2. Calmly ask questions and dig deeper. Here's what your messenger didn't tell you: The sound system doesn't work because half of it's missing. The youth group took it on their weekend retreat.

When you hear bad news, assume it's not the entire story. There may be more bad news, and it's probably worse. Get the *whole* story before you respond.

3. Ask people who bring bad news to your attention what they recommend you do. They've thought about the situation longer than you have, so get their opinion. You don't have to take their advice, but if you've got sharp people on your team, they may have already figured out a solution.

One person on your team might be a policeman who has a megaphone in his trunk. Let the guy preaching the children's sermon use that on Sunday morning, and then meet with the youth pastor on Monday to discuss "borrowing" sound equipment.

FAULTY THOUGHT 4: "I'M ASSUMING THIS IS TRUE—NOBODY TOLD ME OTHERWISE."

When you're a leader and you're trusting information that's not true, you're in deep weeds. Check and double-check your assumptions as you move into and through projects.

Maybe the pastor did say it was fine to have a pet in the children's ministry area so long as you cared for it. But if your pastor imagined a cuddly little hamster, and you haul in a rattlesnake, you'll have a conflict.

A mind-set in which you assume everyone understands what you mean or you assume everyone else shares your vision is a disaster waiting to happen. Don't expect others to read your mind.

Check and double-check. Ask and confirm. You'll sleep better at night, and so will everyone else.

Those four faulty thought patterns can destroy a leader's effectiveness. Avoid them. They're weeds in your garden—pull them and toss them away.

In their place plant the following six attitudes I've observed in outstanding leaders. Cultivate them, and you'll see your leadership flower and bloom.

LEADERSHIP ATTITUDE 1: THINK OF YOURSELF AS A LEADER.

Look in the mirror: Do you see a leader looking back?

Look over your shoulder: Anybody back there counting on you to lead the way?

If God has called you to lead—even if you feel inadequate or uncertain—then *lead*. Use the influence God has given you to help others draw closer to him and to do effective ministry. Decide to be faithful in the role God has given you. See yourself as God sees you.

LEADERSHIP ATTITUDE 2: THINK OF YOURSELF AS A SERVANT—AND SERVE.

Effective leaders don't walk away from problems and challenges—they face them squarely. They don't float through life or walk past broken situations. They get involved.

That's because leaders believe they have something to contribute. Maybe they don't have a quick or easy answer, but they know that they can usually help. They know they're problem solvers.

And more than anything, they know they're here to serve.

In what ways are you involved in your family's life? in your church? your neighborhood? your community?

LEADERSHIP ATTITUDE 3: SEE YOURSELF AS A FOLLOWER, TOO.

It's your job to follow your pastor's lead. If you asked your pastor how well you follow, what would you hear? What you *want* to hear is that you're leading others where the pastor believes God is taking the church.

Some leaders view themselves as trailblazing pioneers, boldly going where no one has gone before. If that's the case, they're going the wrong direction. When faithful leaders lead, God has gone before them and they travel under the authority and with the permission of their pastors.

Leaders are proactive followers, too. Leaders don't shake their heads, wondering, "What were they *thinking*?" when the church board approves a new building campaign. They go find out, so they can get behind the decision.

LEADERSHIP ATTITUDE 4: THINK OUTSIDE THE BOX.

It's great to respect tradition but don't confuse it with Scripture. Be open to new information and methods. Look for better ways to accomplish your purposes and mission.

I'm a middle-aged guy with gray hair, and I'll tell you this: When I started in children's ministry, I didn't approach it the way I approach it today.

Things have changed. There weren't any computers. There wasn't voice mail or e-mail (there was regular mail, but ponies carried it from town to town). Kids didn't think as they think now or hit milestones in their lives as early as they do now. The culture was different. Families were different. *I* was different.

If I'd dug in my heels at any time along the way and quit growing, I'd have quit being an effective leader. You will too.

How flexible is your thinking? How open are you to new ideas and methodologies?

LEADERSHIP ATTITUDE 5: THINK OF CONFLICT AS NATURAL.

We're so worried we'll hurt someone's feelings or that someone will get angry. Effective leaders value people's feelings, but they value moving ahead to get done what God wants done even more.

They know that when you lead, conflict comes with the territory.

The Bible doesn't spell it out, but I'm sure Moses heard all about why some of God's people couldn't leave Egypt. Somebody was sick or too old or about to give birth. Someone had questions about the route. A couple folks had already planned a birthday party, and they didn't want to reschedule.

But when it was time to go, it was time to go. Period. Like it or not, God's people were loading up the donkeys and heading out.

Conflict isn't the worst thing that can happen in your ministry. Apathy is. Conflict is simply an opportunity to get everyone to load up and move out, heading to a better place.

Leadership Attitude 6: Think in organized ways.

It's the details that will trip you up every time. The form you forgot to file. The person you forgot to ask. The curriculum order you forgot to phone in.

Leaders know they won't remember it all, so they keep a running list going. They write things down and cross things off. And they check and double-check whether something got done.

That doesn't mean effective leaders are all naturally organized. Mercy, no! Some of the best leaders I've met have to write things down or they'd never get anything done. These are people who'd panic if they lost their planners. But they care enough about their ministry and the people they serve to get organized and stay that way. They've been willing to learn new skills.

Do you love your ministry and the people you serve enough to take your organizational and management skills to the next level?

I hope so—because as we move through this book that's exactly what you'll have the opportunity to do.

5. Your Role as Leader

No matter how long you're in ministry leadership, you'll always have one person reporting to you who's a problem child. This person will find you on your worst days, test your patience as nobody else, and disappoint you again and again and again.

This person will be next to impossible to manage, but you won't be able to fire him or her. And even if you change churches a dozen times, this person will tag along.

That's because this person is you.

Man, it's true with me. You see, I know what I'm capable of accomplishing. So I know when I didn't give 100 percent to a project. I know when I've rolled over and slept in when I could have gotten up and exercised, building my stamina for service. I know when I stepped up to teach children, and I wasn't well-prepared. Maybe nobody else could tell, but I could.

By far, the worker in my ministry who's toughest to manage is me.

But that's where effective leaders excel: *They manage themselves.* And that gives them the authority to manage others.

If you want to be successful in managing yourself in leadership, a place to begin is by defining your role as a leader. What's your job? What *isn't* your job? Does the job description your church handed you line up with the job description God has given you in Scripture? If not, get your written job description changed right quick; it's going to get in your way, not help you.

First Peter 5:2 says, "Be shepherds of God's flock that is under your care, serving as overseers—not because you must, but because you are willing, as God wants you to be; not greedy for money, but eager to serve."

If you're the leader of a children's ministry, God has handed you two jobs: shepherd and overseer. You've got both those roles to fill, no matter what's on your church's job description.

The Role of Overseer

You're supposed to make sure that stuff gets done—that's what an overseer does. And you're supposed to make sure the flock God has entrusted to you gets fed, watered, and cared for. That's what a shepherd does.

But here's where we get into trouble: When we go into children's ministry, we think the flock we're supposed to oversee are the children. That's probably not the case.

Kids aren't really the majority of your flock. Kids in your ministry are being cared for by the leaders you've trained. *Your* flock is made up of the adults who are shepherding the children. That's who you're working with most closely as you equip them to do ministry.

Huh? Work with grown-ups? But you're in *children's* ministry! Why can't you just go work with kids and let someone else worry about preparing the annual budget, evaluating and training staff, writing the strategic program for outreach, and meeting with the pastor?

Because that's your job, Bub. You're the overseer.

Maybe you always hated math, and you're scared of pulling together a budget. Welcome to the club. Delegate the job of filling in the spreadsheet, but remember it's still your responsibility. You're responsible for creating programs that drive the budget.

Effective overseers don't duck core responsibilities or dodge making key decisions. They stay engaged, even if tasks are delegated. They provide oversight.

Look, if the notion of stepping back from working with kids so you can work with other leaders doesn't sit well with you, I feel your pain. I love to preach to a roomful of kids. I love to teach children. But anymore, preaching and teaching are the easiest things I do in ministry.

What's hard is getting all the stuff done *before* I preach and teach.

Somehow the room has to be prepared—carpets swept, chairs lined up, music selected and rehearsed. Materials have to be chosen, ordered, paid for, and put in the hands of teachers who've been recruited and trained. Decisions have to be made that align the children's ministry with the larger ministry of the church. Somebody has to make all that happen.

And I'll tell you this: It can't always be me.

In fact, it shouldn't be me. I'm an overseer. My job isn't to do everything but to make sure everything gets done. If I'm doing it all myself, I'm not doing my job and I'm crowding other people out of the jobs they're supposed to be doing.

If I could change one thing about children's pastors and other children's ministry leaders, it would be this: They'd learn that *they shouldn't do it alone.*

Time and time again I've visited churches where the children's ministry is a one-person show. There's someone upfront who's doing it all herself. She greets kids at the door, leads the praise and worship time, does the puppet show, and operates the sound and lights. She presents the lesson, sings the special music, then picks up the take-home papers that didn't make it home when the service is over.

When you try to do it all yourself, you are signing up for burnout.

And what's wrong with that? At least she knows everything will be done—and done right. That's the benefit of doing it yourself.

The problem is that because she's doing it alone, she's created an environment where the fruit of her labors won't last. If she leaves, there goes the children's program with her—right out the door.

I get to visit with lots of churches as I speak at conferences. It breaks my heart when I look out at a crowd and realize the same churches as last year are back, but eighty-five percent of the faces are different. The leadership has almost completely turned over because people tried to do it all themselves and burned out. They're gone. And they took the ministries they created with them when they left.

When you try to do it all yourself, you are signing up for burnout. Period. End of story. You simply can't avoid it.

Think about your children's ministry. If you're a one-person show, get used to the idea that you won't last for the long haul.

And here's a question for you: *Why* are you in that spot? Is it because the Lord has surrounded you with talentless, passionless people who won't do ministry? You've tried and tried, but nobody will come alongside you to help?

Or is it that you've not really invited others to participate?

I know this: God hasn't put you in the pool to drown. There's someone somewhere who will carry part of the load you're shouldering. Is there a chance that you're not inviting that person—or those people—to step up and help?

You're to be an overseer. Your job is to find people and equip them for ministry. Your job is *not* to do everything yourself.

Are you willing to be an overseer? to fulfill that administrative, leadership role? to recruit, train, and manage others who'll work with the kids?

Sadly, most children's pastors I know aren't willing to be overseers.

Some of them don't think they have the background, education, or temperament to be in charge. "I don't mind helping out the pastor by running the children's program," they'll say, "but I don't want to be the one who's responsible for the whole thing."

Guess what? You *are* responsible. The question is whether you'll grow into the skills to be effective in meeting that responsibility.

Other children's pastors simply aren't willing to share leg-hugs from boys and girls with anybody else. They want all the attention and glory.

Here's a confession: I'll admit that sometimes I've felt that way. I like having children greet me with those big, around-the-neck hugs. I like having a child draw a picture of me I can stick up on my bulletin board. That feels good.

But I've learned that some of the teachers I've trained are every bit as good a pastor as I am, even if they don't have the title. They like getting those hugs too. When instead of doing it myself, there are three or thirty or three hundred of us doing ministry every week, guess what? A whole lot more ministry gets done. My team doesn't always do ministry exactly the way I'd do it, but that's all right too.

If you're doing it all yourself, make sure it's not because your own perfectionism or ego is in the way of God calling others to get on board.

Remember: It's part of your calling to raise up and train others to do ministry with children. You can't do that if you're unwilling to give up some control.

If you're going to be an overseer, it's time to quit pouring the cups of orange drink before children's church and start pouring your heart for ministry into leaders.

Shepherding the Flock

I believe our first priority as a leader is to feed and care for the sheep God has entrusted to us. I mean, you may run a dozen great programs, but programs aren't going to last forever. Even the best programs will be gone in a few years.

But people? God made people for eternity.

I won't pretend to provide you with everything you need to be an effective people helper. I've got friends who are outstanding pastoral counselors, and they still get stumped frequently. It's a challenge to come alongside people and give them what they need to be contented, growing, faithful sheep. If you're overwhelmed at the thought of guiding your volunteers into a deeper relationship with God, you're probably right. You *should* feel overwhelmed—and let that send you straight to God for strength and guidance.

Be an overseer who equips others to do shepherding.

Finally, when you're managing your role as leader, don't forget to take care of this…

Managing Your Workload

I've got some bad news for you: You have limitations. You can't do everything. Sooner or later you've got to rest.

I see you smiling. Maybe it's because you don't really believe that. You thrive on the energy of ministry or doing the impossible. You'd pull three all-nighters in a row if you could figure out how to sleep with your eyes open.

Fatigue is part of the cost of being in ministry, right?

No, it isn't. And when you try to stretch yourself too thin, you end up hurting other people in addition to hurting yourself.

I was on a three-hour flight with a guy whose company supplies T-shirts and wearable accessories for Disney. This guy ran his multimillion dollar business from an office high in the Empire State Building. When it came to financial security, he'd arrived.

I was telling him about going shopping with my daughters, and he laughed. "I never shop with my kids. My secretary does the shopping for me."

I probed a bit, and he finally explained that he couldn't take them shopping, even if he'd wanted to do it. "My kids hate my guts," he admitted. "Even my wife hates my guts."

How sad. He'd poured his life into building his company, but he'd lost his family in the process.

I wish I could tell you that never happens in the ministry, but it does. All the time. So many family tragedies could be avoided if people like you and me would manage our workload.

Don't count on your supervisor and pastor to set your limits for you. It'd be nice if they noticed and helped you work reasonable hours, but they might not notice you're headed for burnout until it's too late. Don't expect the people you serve to tell you to slow down, either. It's up to you.

It's your responsibility to manage yourself and your workload. The next few chapters will give you some ideas for how to do just that.

6. Managing Your Time

Of all the resources you can spend to accomplish things, time is the most valuable. Why? Because it's the only one you can't get more of.

If you run over budget, you can always ask the church treasurer for a few extra bucks. But the hours you've spent are gone. So it makes sense for you to make the most of time—yours and that of your staff and volunteers.

I'm not suggesting you get a stranglehold on your time so you can do nothing but work. I know people like that—they rush between meetings with a cellular phone in one hand and a hamburger in the other.

The goal of time management isn't to set a new world's record for how much you can get done. It's to figure out how to get done the most important stuff—and that includes time off.

Here's a truth: People who manage their time well can work fewer hours, not more. They aren't rushing to the church at midnight to take care of something they forgot to do. They know what projects are going well and which ones are in trouble—*before* a crisis develops.

If you get your time under control, you can take off more days and still get things done.

Four Keys to Managing Your Time

Here are four skills that will help you get more done than you thought humanly possible.

1. PLAN YOUR TIME.

Get yourself a good calendar, and write down how you want to spend your time. Fill it in a year in advance or longer if possible.

You know you're going to have a VBS, so why not decide now where it'll fit on the calendar next summer and the summer after that?

First, enter usually scheduled events. The programs you know are coming, the holidays, everything you know already. Get them all down so you know at a glance when you're likely to be busy.

Now add other things you need to remember: holidays, school holidays, and school breaks. The children in our church come from districts with four different spring breaks. That's handy information when I'm figuring out when to have our first session of camp!

Write down staff retreats and planning sessions, too. If you meet regularly with your church board or pastor, get those down on the calendar. Write down every recurring meeting you're expected to attend.

Finally, put in your anniversary, the birthdays of family members, and if you usually go on vacation the same time each year, get that down.

Your calendar is pretty full, isn't it? Well, it's about to get *more* full.

Now figure out the deadlines you'll need to hit to get you ready for each event. If your Fall Kickoff is the first week of September, you'll need to order supplies in August. If you want to rent an inflatable game, you'd better call and reserve it in March. Fill in the steps you need to take to pull off each event.

I hear you: "Brother Jim, I'm just not that organized. I can't keep all those steps straight."

Hey—I'm not that kind of person either. That's why I use a calendar. Lord knows enough things come up that I can't possibly plan for, so I want to plan those I *can* plan. Then the only thing I have to do is check my calendar every day, and I've got a hope of being organized. I don't want to find myself two weeks before the Fall Kickoff realizing it's too late to pull it together.

Don't put your calendar away yet because you're about to add the really important stuff. You can't afford to miss appointments with…

THE LORD—I'm not spiritual enough to get up at 5:30 a.m. every day to pray and read the Bible. It's not going to happen. But 3:00 p.m. works for me. If someone calls and says, "Can I meet you at 3:00?" I say, "I already have an appointment then. How about 4:00?" Nobody gets offended.

Do not skip reserving time for prayer. Being faithful to know, love, and follow God is the most important thing you can do with your time!

YOUR FAMILY—I'm a family man before I'm a children's pastor, so I put birthdays on my work calendar. My anniversary is there. So are piano recitals, dates with my wife and daughters, and other significant family events. I block off that time, and I defend it.

My family members don't get offended if they see I've scheduled an appointment with them. That doesn't mean I'm unavailable other times; it means that in addition to wanting to be with them other times, I've made a point to be available at special times.

DAILY LIFE—There are things in your life that will take time next month. You don't know what they all are just yet, but they'll show up, guaranteed.

If you've booked every hour solid, what will you do when a toothache gets your attention? When your car breaks down? When a child needs you? Smart time managers don't schedule each and every hour; they anticipate interruptions and crises and leave time to deal with them.

Do this: Block out a few hours each day and write down "people." Sometimes those people will be master teachers who want coaching, your pastor who has a great idea to discuss, or your daughter who needs some hugging after losing a volleyball game. Build in room for interruptions.

LEADERS YOU'RE HELPING TO DEVELOP—I reserve lunches to meet with people who report to me and whom I'm discipling. And I don't just meet people at restaurants. If at all possible, I arrange to go with them to the place we're eating. That gives us more time together. We can talk openly in the car without worrying if someone can overhear us. That can be a problem in a restaurant.

2. PREPARE.

This is where you quit writing down what you want to accomplish and get busy figuring out how to make sure you get it done. You've already backed into deadlines on your calendar, but how will you make sure you do them?

Carrying a to-do list goes a long way in helping you manage your time. It can be as simple as an index card you tuck into your pocket or as cool as an electronic organizer. Check it often during the day, so you can stay on track.

What forms do you need to get that monthly expense report turned in? How will you collect numbers, mileage, and receipts? Put systems in place, or you'll never get it done.

Good preparation is the step that separates calendar-keepers from *effective* calendar-keepers. And this is the place to ask a question: Did you *really* fill in the step-by-step deadlines that will help you get next year's VBS done in a timely fashion? If you didn't, go back and do it now.

When will you pick a theme? order curriculum for review? meet with your VBS publicity chairman and your recruitment chairman? When will you train volunteers? start the sign-ups?

Sort out the tasks in logical order, and get them on your calendar. Otherwise, your planning calendar isn't worth much. Reminders really make a big difference.

3. EVALUATE HOW YOU'RE USING YOUR TIME.

This is when you stop writing down how you want to spend your time and start writing down how you actually spent it.

> **Most calls can comfortably be ended in five minutes or less.**

Trust me: This exercise will open your eyes. You don't even need a calendar; just keep a running log going on a sheet of paper.

How much time did you talk on the phone—exactly? with whom and about what? How much time did you spend watching TV, and what shows did you watch? Were they work related or goof-off related?

"But Brother Jim, I *have* to watch the news."

No, you don't. I gave up watching the news when my daughters were little so I could play Barbie dolls with them. I asked myself: Is it more important to know who is bombing whom or whether Whitney had a good day in school?

Now my daughters don't play Barbies anymore; they *look* like Barbies. And I still want to know how they're doing. When I quit caring about that, I'll have more time for television.

The reason to evaluate how you spend your time is so you can spend it the way God wants you to spend it. Remember—you won't get even one minute back. You've got to be a good steward of time.

When you check your week's log, look for time wasters—tasks that didn't help you accomplish anything worthwhile. Were you focused or just filling hours?

If you'll save one hour per day, over the course of a year you'll free up two full weeks of twenty-four-hour days. That's forty-two eight-hour work-days. That's some powerful motivation.

Here's what I do: Every night before I go to bed, I look back at the day. I ask myself how I used my time and what I can change that will make me more efficient the next day.

One night I walked by a pay phone with a sign taped above it that read: "Please limit business calls to 3 minutes."

It dawned on me: The phone on my desk at church is a business phone. When I pick up the phone, I flip a switch on a timer that's set for five minutes. I do my level best to end that call before the buzzer sounds.

It's not that I want to be mean or cold; it's that I want to be efficient. Most calls can comfortably be ended in five minutes or less—the rest of the time is wasted. This habit has saved me hundreds of hours to use elsewhere.

Every night I also ask myself how to be more effective the next day. What should I be focusing on? What needs to be accomplished first?

Again—the idea behind managing your time isn't to figure out ways to squeeze more activities into the day. The goal is to do the right things and to do them efficiently. That's good stewardship.

4. USE THE TIME OF OTHERS.

What are you doing that someone else could do? What are you doing that's keeping you from doing what *only* you can do?

It dawned on me one day that I'm not the only guy who can cue up the puppet tapes. I realized my Sundays were packed with things that others would gladly do—if I'd delegate the responsibility and authority to handle those tasks.

Here's what I've learned about using the time of others:

REQUEST WEEKLY REPORTS.

What numbers does your pastor want to see each week? attendance? giving? conversions? Ask volunteers to provide those numbers to you from their areas of ministry. And decide what else you want to know.

I have four questions I ask my paid staff every week:

1. What things did you accomplish this week?

2. What did you do for leadership development?

3. Is there anything you know that *I* need to know?

4. Is there anything I know that *you* need to know?

Four simple questions—but the answers tell me what's happening, what information people need, and what my staff is doing to grow.

And the answers to those four questions help me assist my staff in setting priorities for the coming week. I know what they're planning, so I can provide guidance to keep their priorities lined up with my priorities…and my pastor's.

COMMUNICATE IN WRITING WHENEVER POSSIBLE.

Churches have way too many meetings. We even meet to vote on which meetings we need!

Almost every volunteer I know can read, so I send memos, letters, e-mail, and faxes. I go out of my way to avoid meetings, which means:

1. We have time to get some real work done, and
2. When I *do* call a meeting, people know it's important—so they show up.

I don't hold monthly volunteer meetings because it's a waste of time to pull everyone together when I really want to talk just to the registration workers or the new teachers. I'm selective about who I invite to meetings—and we cover specific material aimed just at them.

Use these tips to keep meetings from consuming your calendar (and life!):

- **Schedule as many meetings as possible during the day, not in the evening.** Ask people to meet you for breakfast. It costs a few dollars, but you'll keep your evening free for family.

- **If you must have an evening meeting, schedule it on a night that people are already coming to church.** It minimizes strain on your volunteers—and you.

- **There's no such thing as a perfect meeting time.** There's always someone who can't make it. Always have a plan for distributing information to no-shows.

- **Provide food.** Volunteers appreciate it when you say, "Just come early to church, and I'll feed you and your kids." They have to eat anyway, so meeting over a mealtime isn't a big deal.

- **Plan recurring meetings the same time each month.** It helps the planning-impaired people on your team.

- **Be efficient.** Advertise a starting time and an ending time. Start on time. End on time. Never run over. If you realize you can't cover everything on your agenda, cut items from your agenda.

- **Allow time for questions.** If a question doesn't pertain to the whole group or the subject being discussed, address the question privately following the meeting. Stay as long as you're needed. Realize that sometimes people won't ask a question or make a comment in front of others.

- **Make sure people know what they're to do.** Before you adjourn the meeting, repeat clearly the action steps and assignments that have been given during the meeting.

- **Don't waste people's time.** When conducting a meeting that includes people from different areas of responsibility, first go over the agenda items that pertain to the whole group. Then dismiss everyone who isn't involved with the other agenda items.

WHEN YOU MUST HAVE A MEETING, DISTRIBUTE AN AGENDA IN ADVANCE.

Agendas help you stay on task at meetings. They eliminate rambling and keep everyone focused. And advance agendas help people prepare.

Do this for me: If someone invites you to a meeting, request an agenda upfront. How else can you know whether or not you should attend?

Of course, if it's your pastor calling the meeting, just go. Your pastor *is* the agenda.

DON'T TREAT ALL VOLUNTEERS EQUALLY.

Here's a harsh fact that bothers some children's ministry leaders: It's smart to play favorites among volunteers.

Jesus didn't spend an equal amount of time with each disciple. Peter, James, and John got way more than their "fair share" of Jesus' time. And maybe now and then the other disciples got jealous.

But Jesus invested his time in people who moved his mission and purpose forward. He never apologized for having an "inner circle." You don't need to apologize either.

Not every volunteer wants to spend more time with you. Some are already booked solid, and others aren't interested in deepening their skills and commitment. They're marginal volunteers.

But there are people who want training and discipleship. They want to grow. They want to stick with serving in children's ministry. They're where you can most profitably invest your time.

Who are the people in your inner circle?

MAKE PEOPLE TAKE TIME OFF.

Sometimes I tell people who work with me, "Go home. You shouldn't be here at this hour." I literally throw them out of the building for a day or two.

Volunteers will work themselves into a state of exhaustion thinking they're helping you or the church and that they're honoring God. When they burn out and drop out of ministry, we shake our heads and wonder why.

I'll tell you why: *They're tired!* Children's ministry is a marathon, not a one-hundred-yard dash. You're in it for the long haul, not just until VBS ends. Even convicts get time off for good behavior. Shouldn't the people you direct?

MAKE THINGS EASY FOR YOUR STAFF AND VOLUNTEERS.

Offer help. Streamline and simplify procedures. Look for ways you can make serving in your children's ministry painless.

Now and then I ask my staff, "What should we kill?" A program that's become too hard to pull off? a complicated curriculum? What could we change that will make doing ministry quicker, easier, or cheaper?

Ask people who work in the trenches what would make their lives easier. When I'm considering how to change the nursery check-in policies, I don't make that decision myself. I call up the little old lady who does it week after week and say, "If you were in charge, what sort of changes would you make?"

Then I do what she says. She knows. She's living it. She's got a better handle on the nursery than you have as you sit in your office.

FIND EQUIPMENT AND TECHNOLOGY THAT HELPS YOUR TEAM.

I've just found the neatest thing: a wireless keyboard. Now I can go into a church and hook up to their video system and control presentation slides myself. No more hauling a projector with me. No more hoping the sound guy shows up.

This is technology that solves my problems, and, boy, I love it.

What technology could solve your volunteers' problems? Would a computer system make the check-in table hum along at three times the speed? Would a new CD player down in children's church take 90 percent of the stress out of your music leader's life?

Provide the tools your people need to be effective and efficient. You'll have happier people, and they'll have more time to be available.

MOVE PAST DELEGATION TO DUPLICATION.

It's good when you delegate. Then you've got someone representing you and acting on your behalf.

But *duplication* is even better. That's when your staff members can do what you can do. They have your heart for ministry. You've coached them until they're a copy of the original—you.

There's no success without a successor. Who's your successor? Who can do what you do and maybe do it better? And who is *that* person training? If you don't know, it's probably not happening.

If there were two of you, you'd have way more time to meet your ministry goals. Well, there's no reason there can't be two of you...or twenty!

Top Ten List for Mastering Time Management

Here's a quick list of the skills you need to be a certified time management marvel.

10. Account for your time. Do you know how you spent your day? Write it down and evaluate it.

9. Plan your time offensively. Remember: Your time belongs to you. Make a to-do list. Don't automatically say yes when someone asks you for a meeting.

8. Keep your priorities in order. Administer triage with every situation that comes your way. Deal with the big stuff first and the timely stuff first.

7. Delegate to faithful, capable people. What are you doing that someone else could do? Teach someone how to do it, then check in to ensure success.

6. Plan for interruptions. Things won't go exactly as planned; leave room in your schedule to deal with surprises.

5. Respond rather than react to crises. There are always two (or more) sides to a story. Stay calm and get the facts—*then* make a decision.

4. Don't procrastinate. Don't put off the things you dread.

3. Get help. You don't have all the answers, so find some people who can help you get them. Make a call. Read a book. Seek out a mentor.

2. Plan for growth. People follow a leader who has a plan. What's your plan for growing spiritually, organizationally, and numerically?

1. Pray. Things happen in you and in your ministry when you pray that won't happen any other way.

7. Your Roles, Priorities, and Goals

It's easy to feel intimidated when you start thinking about roles, priorities, and goals. They sound so important and permanent.

Let me make it easy for you with a seven-step process:

1. Identify your roles in life.

Maybe you're a parent, a son or daughter, a husband or wife, a Christian, and a leader. You may also be a student and a small group leader. Those are all roles. Write down all the roles you fill in life, in any order they come to mind.

This is a book for children's ministry leaders, but "children's ministry leader" is probably just one role on a very long list. You might wonder why I'm asking you to write down *all* your roles.

I've seen ministry leaders practically ignore their own families so they can help other families at church. They miss their own kids' piano recitals so they can attend others' kids' events. A person can do a great job filling the "children's leader" role, but the role as "parent" can suffer terribly.

I think it helps to look at all your roles—everything you could be doing—so you can decide which roles are most important. You're just human. You can't do everything, so you have to make choices.

2. Circle the important roles.

I know: Your roles are all important. That's why you're doing them.

But they're not all equally important.

Circle any role you listed that only *you* can do. For instance, if you have "volunteer firefighter" and "mother" listed, circle "mother." That's because no matter how important it is to be a volunteer firefighter, someone else could do it. But nobody else can be your child's mother.

Now circle any role that is absolutely required to faithfully follow God. It's your purpose in life to be faithful, so let's make sure "Christian" is circled. And if you're called to children's ministry, circle "children's ministry leader" or however else you identified that role.

Just because "square dancer" isn't circled doesn't mean you can never do-si-do again. A balanced life includes doing some things just for fun or exercise.

But when push comes to shove, the roles you've circled are the really important ones—your gotta-do list. Everything else is icing on the cake. That might mean you give up square dancing, at least for this season in your life.

For me, I had to step back from music. I *love* playing guitar. I went to the Rock and Roll Hall of Fame in Cleveland and wanted to just move on in. On my list of roles in life, you'll find "GUITAR PLAYER" in big, block letters.

But I'm also a daddy. And a husband. And several other things that require time and energy. I just can't justify sitting in my den practicing three hours a day and playing in a band every weekend.

So for now I work when I should and I play when the opportunity arises. "GUITAR PLAYER" is still on my role list, but it's down toward the bottom.

3. Pray about your circled roles.

Get a fresh sheet of paper, and list your circled roles. These are the roles in life that will define you, and it's time to do some soul searching.

You need to know if your must-do roles, as you see them, match up with what God wants you to be doing. God's plan often differs from our own plans.

Proverbs 14:12 says "There is a way that seems right to a man, but in the end it leads to death." There are some serious consequences to missing God's plan for our lives.

Do your roles line up with the Word of God? If you've got a spouse and your role of husband or wife isn't circled, you're in trouble, and not just with your spouse. You're in trouble with God, who joined you and your spouse together. He expects you to do everything possible to protect and nurture that marriage relationship. It's important.

Paul writes in 2 Corinthians 5:9 about whom we need to be pleasing most: God. "So we make it our goal to please him, whether we are at home in the body or away from it."

Pray about your list. Do the roles you've chosen honor and please God?

4. Decide how you'll live out your roles.

Now it's time to define your roles.

If you've written "mother," jot down ideas for what it means to be a first-rate mom. Does it mean being involved in your child's education? serving on the PTA? home schooling? Ask God to guide you as you dream about filling that role with excellence.

Clarify every role you circled. What's it mean to be an excellent children's ministry worker? Are you a doer or a leader? a coach and trainer or a teacher in the classroom? Get it down on paper.

Talk about this with people who matter to you. Ask your kids how they define an excellent parent. What does your spouse think it means to be an excellent husband or wife? Ask your boss what it means to be an excellent employee.

And ask your pastor to define what it means to be an excellent ministry leader. Why? Because you're at the church to serve your pastor, so it's just smart to find out if your ideas line up with your pastor's ideas.

Spend time getting role definitions down on paper because those definitions are your marching orders.

Here's how it works: Suppose you circled "parent" as a top role. And you decided that "being actively involved in shaping the spiritual life of my children" is one part of how you define that role. So how do you accomplish that?

You could start by making sure you get your kids to church, but that's not enough. You might also decide to talk with your children daily about how they saw God working in their lives. You may decide a time of family prayer each day will help you shape their hearts for God.

Those three specific action steps will help you fill the role of parent with excellence. You'll probably come up with another thirty things you could do…but you can't do them all, all the time.

So do this: Circle the five or six most important things you could do to fill your parent role with excellence. If on a busy day, you can only squeeze in five or six of your thirty or forty action steps, which five or six would you pick?

Those are your top priorities. They're the things you most want to do—and they'll help you fill roles God wants you to fill.

See how going through this process helps you have a purposeful, focused life? You'll identify and do the most important things to fill your most important roles. You can make a difference in the lives you touch.

5. Look to the next week...month...and year.

How will you stay on target and focus on your top priorities—those actions that help you fill important roles? Life's full of distractions, and it's easy to quit doing what's important because you're taking care of urgent things.

You stay on target by creating—and meeting—goals.

A goal is a statement describing what you want to accomplish. "I want to be an excellent parent" is a goal—but not a very useful one. For a goal to actually help you accomplish one of your priorities, it has to include these elements:

- It's specific. "I want to be an excellent parent *by tucking my child into bed*" is specific.

- It's measurable. You can tell if you've tucked a child into bed. You've either done it or you haven't.

- It's attainable. You can actually do it. "I'll flap my arms and fly to Toledo" is a goal, but I doubt you can do it.

- It's time oriented. "I want to be an excellent parent by tucking my child into bed *at least five times a week*" is realistic and time oriented. You can write the activity on a calendar to remind you to do it until it becomes a habit.

Do this: For each of your top priorities, set some goals. You want to be an excellent parent? Tucking your child into bed five nights a week might be an appropriate goal. So might taking the child to church at least once per week. Set goals that support your priorities, and tweak them until they're specific, measurable, attainable, and time oriented.

Write the goals onto your calendar and to-do list so you actually complete the tasks. They're helping you live out your most important God-given roles. What else is more important to do each day?

6. Find someone to hold you accountable.

It may be your pastor or a supervisor, a mentor or your spouse. Friends are great accountability partners if they're willing to tell you the truth—and you're honest with them.

Give this person—or these people—a copy of your top roles, your priorities (what has to happen to do the roles with excellence), and your goals (specific action steps to help you accomplish your priorities). Ask people who are holding you accountable to check in with you every month to find out where you need help and where you need prayer.

7. Write a date in your calendar to revisit this process.

Things change, so decide now when you'll go back through this process. The second, third, and fourth time through won't take as long, and it's worth the effort. I suggest you revise your roles and priorities or decide to leave them the same once a year.

Don't mistake activity for making progress.

You'll have to revisit your *goals* far more often. Sometimes the things you need to do to be an excellent ministry leader change quickly, and the changes aren't initiated by you.

When I came to work with Pastor Willie George at Church on the Move, I quickly learned to listen for three words Pastor Willie says on a regular basis: "I've been thinking…"

When Pastor Willie says, "I've been thinking," it means that we're fixing to get *real* busy, *real* soon. My goals are about to change.

Sometimes those three words mean "third service coming." Or "more bus routes." Or "add more staff." It's amazing how those three words get translated differently each time he says them. And no matter how they're translated, my goals shift immediately.

But guess what? He's the pastor. I work to support his ministry. He can rearrange my work priorities anytime he wants. And it's fun to work for someone who has a vision for growth. When I came on board, we had about twelve hundred people in the church. A little more than twelve years later, we have twelve hundred people in our preschool ministry alone.

When you work for a pastor who has a vision for excellence and growth, you won't get bored. You'll hear yourself pray what I pray daily: "Lord, just let me keep up."

I know establishing your roles, priorities, and goals takes effort. But if you're clear on them you can be effective in your work.

You see, you can be very busy in doing ministry work and still not accomplish a blessed thing. Don't mistake activity for making progress. Being busy isn't a virtue—we've got to be busy doing the right things.

Post your list of top priorities where you'll see it often. When you look at your priorities, ask yourself which ones need immediate attention, which ones are long-range goals and can take some time for action, and which ones may no longer be relevant. As your children grow older and leave home, your "I'll parent with excellence" priority and goals will certainly change. Other priorities can shift, too.

As an example, let me share a list of my roles and priorities. I also have goals that fit under my priorities, but that list is too long to include.

1. Follower of Jesus Christ

I will follow, worship, obey, and love God.

2. Husband

I will be a faithful husband to Julie, and I will be a loving man she's proud to have as a husband.

3. Father

I will be a father who instills God's principles in the lives of Yancy and Whitney and be a support and guide in their development.

4. Children's pastor (I've expanded this section so you can see how I'm defining my ministry.)

I'll help my pastor, Willie George, to implement his God-given vision for Church on the Move. I'll be a faithful servant and an excellent staff member.

I'll reflect the Lord's heart, as expressed in Matthew 12:47-50, to my department heads, who I will coach, care for, and confront, ever seeking to encourage these servants to excellence.

I'll champion the following ministry goals:

Corporate: I will enthusiastically embrace the church's vision statement.

Christian education department: I will mold the children's department to support and advance the church's vision statement.

Individual: I will perform my duties with excellence and continually grow in my skills.

Personal:

• I will be a man of God in every part of my life.
• I will love and do the Word of God.
• I will be a godly husband.
• I will be a loving father.
• I will be an able minister and lover of people.
• I will be a leaders' leader in word and example.
• I will help children in my care fulfill the callings on their lives.
• I will be healthy and in good physical condition.
• I will be a soul winner.
• I will train those in my ministry to be soul winners.

- I will lead and administrate a local church's children's ministry that pastors over ten thousand people weekly.
- I will recruit, train, and maintain a teaching staff of over twenty-five hundred leaders.
- I will train and encourage over fifty thousand children's ministers annually through seminars, conferences, and teaching tapes.
- I will provide helpful, anointed, quality products for children's and youth ministry including books, music tapes, teaching tapes, and teaching videos.
- I will personally mentor twenty leaders who can and will become better leaders than I am.

8. Maintaining Your Integrity

Being a leader isn't the same thing as being a politician.

There are politicians who never quite tell you what they're going to do. Or they tell you what you want to hear. You learn right quick that their promises don't mean much.

That approach to working with people may get someone elected, but it doesn't make you an effective leader in the church.

Ministry leaders need to have integrity, to line up with God's Word, and to do what they say they'll do. It's essential...but it's not always the way people in leadership do business.

Lying—and let's call a *lack of integrity* what it really is—can smooth out a rough situation. It can help you avoid conflict. It can oil a squeaky wheel. And it can also become a habit that destroys your character and ministry.

Do this: Listen to yourself for the next few days. Are you in the habit of telling people only what they want to hear? leaving out key facts? slanting the truth? Has that habit of compromise gotten hold of you?

Are you authentic—the same person when you're with church people as you are when you're alone or off on a business trip? Does your leadership depend on people not knowing what you truly believe? not knowing what you look at when you're flipping through the cable channels or surfing the Net?

If so, repent, my friend. Talk to the Lord about it, and also talk to your pastor or another trusted person. Give your heart and habits to God. Get your own house in order before trying to lead others.

Don't think you're fooling people. You may get along for a while, but they'll figure you out. And God will know all along.

And you know who else is quick to spot a phony? Children.

I learned a long time ago that if I promise *children* something, I'd better deliver. That's why I hate outdoor activities in children's ministry—I can't control the weather. It takes just one good thunderstorm to cancel a picnic, parade, or carnival.

Here's an example of how making a promise got me in a *lot* of trouble…

We decided to drop Easter eggs in a field behind our church building. Not real Easter eggs; instead we bought seventeen thousand individually wrapped marshmallow eggs. We chartered a helicopter from which to lob them down on the thousands of kids I was sure would show up for this event.

The field in back of our building was bordered on one side by a subdivision, by a horse pasture on the opposite side, and on the third side by a huge oak tree.

We advertised for weeks. On the day of the event, the field was full of kids. It was also full of gusting wind, courtesy of an approaching storm. I received word that the helicopter was grounded at the airport.

Thousands of kids, seventeen thousand Easter eggs, and no way to get them together. I had a problem.

What could I do? I'd promised an egg drop so I had to deliver one—no matter what.

The pilot scratched his head and offered to fly a small plane he owned instead of the helicopter. The plane wasn't grounded, even with high winds in the area. The pilot couldn't make a precise drop, but *if* he made a couple passes to calculate the drift of the eggs and *if* his brother hung out the window to lob the eggs—it might work.

What choice did I have? I agreed, and within thirty minutes a tiny plane sputtered into view over the field of upturned, grinning faces.

On the first pass, the pilot's brother emptied a box of eggs out of the door, and the eggs caught a wind gust. Over in the subdivision, eggs *shelled* everything: cars, roofs, and yards. People exploded out of their houses to find out why they were under attack.

During the second pass, as the plane dove, the horses decided *they* were under attack. They went berserk, ripping back and forth, wild-eyed and frantic. But the eggs hit the target. Kids were *scrambling* for eggs.

That's when someone pointed at the plane. Apparently the pilot was concentrating so hard on the egg drop that he'd forgotten about the big oak tree. He was racing straight at it, his brother hanging out the window and pointing.

The good news: The pilot missed the tree. By inches.

The bad news: Between aggravated neighbors and an irate horse owner, the Federal Aviation Administration got so many phone calls they pulled the pilot's license for a time. And our neighbors weren't any too thrilled with us either.

I'd kept my promise to the kids, but at a high, high price. I'd have been smarter to schedule something that didn't require blue skies and mild weather.

Integrity requires we keep our promises. That the children and adults we serve know that we mean what we say and do what we promise to do. But even beyond that, integrity demands we be authentic—including a willingness to admit it when we've made mistakes.

> # Temptations don't go away because you move into leadership. If anything, the devil attacks you with even greater intensity when you're a leader.

Integrity isn't always easy.

Consider Joseph. In Genesis 39–41, we read about a guy who, after a rough start, was doing all the right stuff. He was living with integrity, but just the same he got in trouble.

Joseph worked his way into a position of authority and then was tempted to commit adultery. When he refused, he ended up in prison.

Joseph had every earthly right to be bitter. He'd done the right thing—and look where it got him! But Joseph praised God and saw God's hand in what had happened. That was another piece of his integrity: Joseph worshipped God all the time, not just when things went well.

I believe there are lots of reasons leaders fail—and at the core many of them involve a lack of integrity. I'm not just talking about outright lying on a resume or falling into sexual sin. I'm talking about cutting corners. About sliding into a habit you wouldn't want your pastor to know about. About entertaining thoughts that fall way short of honoring God.

Remember: No ministry leader sets out to fail.

But again and again, leaders who start out strong, crash and burn. After a few years, they're out of the ministry. Or they're still in ministry, but they're no longer leading.

What happened? And how can you keep it from happening to you?

I think it comes down to standing firm when you're tempted to set aside your integrity. Temptations don't go away because you move into leadership. If anything, the devil attacks you with even greater intensity when you're a leader. That means you, friend, are under attack. You'd better be praying—and asking others to pray for you.

If you're like most leaders I've met, you're not immune to the following "integrity temptations." They're there every day, so every day you need to ask God for strength to turn to him instead of elsewhere.

How are you doing with the following temptations?

THE TEMPTATION TO BE SELF-SUFFICIENT

We get a few years of ministry under our belts and think we've got this ministry thing nailed. We read through the Bible or get our Bible degree and think we know it all. We pray at meals but let our personal devotion times slip. We start thinking God doesn't have anything more to tell us.

We start walking in our own power, thinking that being successful is better than being faithful. We're such good planners that we forget to ask God what he wants us to do.

If you're a Christian leader, you'll never be self-sufficient. Never. Not for one day. You are where you are to serve God and do what he wants done. If you're in leadership for any other reason, move aside or repent.

Integrity demands that you see yourself as God's servant—relying on him all the time, not just when people are watching.

THE TEMPTATION TO BE LAZY

We begin telling ourselves, "I've paid my dues. I've worked long and hard, so now I'll coast a bit."

We lose our passion. We lose our first love. We lose focus. We become caretakers, not leaders.

We're like those pastors who just rotate through old sermons they've used in other places. We're not doing anything new or pushing for the change God wants to see in us and in our churches.

Now, I'm all for slowing down now and then to rest. I read Genesis and I think there's a good theological justification for taking a day off each and every week. And if you've just gotten through a month of rehearsals and performances for a children's program, then you might need to slow down for a while.

But that's different from deciding that you can back off from the fundamentals of leadership that make you effective.

Have you become lazy or complacent in your work? Are you excited or bored? faithful or fading? When you encourage others to do their best for the Lord, are you speaking with integrity?

THE TEMPTATION TO COMPROMISE ON MORAL ISSUES

Things that were once black and white become gray. You once had ministry friends who honestly knew you, but you don't meet with them anymore. You aren't transparent with your mentors or your pastor any longer. You know you're hiding something.

It's not that you've gone out and murdered anyone. But you've taken the first few steps toward becoming someone who you don't respect. And the thought of taking the next few steps doesn't seem so bad.

Are you lying to yourself? avoiding certain subjects when you talk to God? avoiding time alone with God? Do you have a godly friend who knows you thoroughly—who knows even the stuff you don't want anyone else to know? Who? Have you given this person permission to speak truth into your life? Are you listening?

The devil doesn't need to convince you to do something horrible to knock you and your leadership off the tracks. All the devil needs to do is help you do something that causes you to feel shame. Once that happens, you'll pull yourself out of the game and set yourself on the bench where you're no good as a leader.

Do you feel shame about anything? Deal with it before God and a friend who loves both you and God, and arrange to spend regular time with that friend. Let that friend share with you the reassuring words God wants you to hear.

THE TEMPTATION TO LEAVE YOUR CALLING AND CHURCH

Has God called you to ministry? to minister in the spot you're serving right now? If so, why are you considering leaving just because things are tough?

I'll never forget the time at my church in Montgomery when a little girl spotted the senior pastor and me walking down a hall. Her eyes lit up, and she yelled, "Pastor!" as she came running down the hall. My senior pastor leaned down and opened his arms, but she zipped right past him to give me a hug.

My pastor looked up at me and grinned. "Well, I guess I know where *I* stand," he said.

It could have been a terrible moment, but a little later he said to me, "I'm so proud of the relationship you have with the boys and girls in this congregation." He understood how to love people, and he was willing to share the limelight with me.

That's the sort of pastor you want to serve under. A pastor who values serving children. Who values you. When you find a pastor like that, it's a joy to be in charge of the children's ministry.

But what if that's not the spot you're in right now?

I remember when I first served in children's ministry. We'd grown from a handful of kids to a crowd of three hundred children. As I prayed about what direction to head next, I received a vision about my ministry. I saw myself equipping leaders and influencing churches.

I asked the senior pastor for a meeting so I could bring him up to date. It turned out he also wanted to meet with me.

He started by leading me on a walk around the church property. He pointed out where he saw new buildings going up on the campus to support new ministries. And he said, "You know, I never really wanted the children's ministry to get this big. I'd like you to focus more on adult ministry and quit spending so much time with the kids. And someday when I retire, well, I think maybe you'll be ready to be the senior pastor."

I was stunned. When he turned to me and said, "Now what was on your mind?" my answer came out as a surprise, even to me.

"I'll be leaving."

I'd assumed that the new level of leadership and service God called me to would happen at that church. I was rock-solid certain I was supposed to labor in the field of children's ministry. And that meant I couldn't shift my focus as my pastor requested.

I believe you work for the pastor. It's your job to find out what the pastor wants and to deliver it. But if God's specific call in your life won't let you follow your pastor's vision for ministry or leadership, then step aside so someone else can fill your spot.

Even if you aren't sure where you'll go next.

Look, ministry is hard. There are people who will not embrace or follow you no matter what you say or do. There are situations that will grind you down if you let them. There are problems that are beyond your control to fix.

Believe it or not, sometimes the people who challenge your leadership most don't do it because of you. It's nothing personal. They're trying to get at your pastor through you. Or they don't think children's ministry should get so much attention and support. Or they're mad about something totally unrelated to you or your ministry, and you're just in the line of fire.

But God is still God. He's still with you. And he's still good all the time—no matter how you feel. No matter what you've done—or are considering doing—he's calling you back into a close walk with him.

So are you on the track—or derailed?

And what are you going to do about it?

9. Delegation

I was audited by the Internal Revenue Service several years ago.

It wasn't all that bad. I won my auditor to the Lord, which made the experience worthwhile all by itself, and, as a bonus, I found out what other people think we do as children's ministry leaders.

The auditor could understand me wanting to write off a new Bible—that made sense. But clown makeup? balloons? food for kids? What did they have to do with children's ministry?

It took some explaining on my part. Ministering to kids involves stuff. *Lots* of stuff. Stuff to snag kids' attention, to illustrate Bible points, and to entertain them while you're sharing the gospel.

And food? I thought everyone knew the cardinal rule of ministry to kids: If you feed them, they will come. The IRS wasn't familiar with that concept, but I've straightened them out. You can thank me for it if you ever get audited yourself.

The fact is that working with children takes a lot of skills. You've got to be a teacher, a preacher, and it helps if you're also a musician. You should know your way around a few illusionist tricks, too, and be a stand-up comic. A degree from clown college isn't a bad idea, and you'd better be up to speed in drama, mime, ventriloquism, cartooning, storytelling, arts and crafts, and puppetry.

No wonder you're tired!

Oh, and you also need to be an expert in visitation and pastoral care, advertising and marketing, and be a liaison with social agencies in your community. You've got to know the law as it relates to children and families.

And then there's dealing with audio and video activities, and photography. These days you're sunk without computer and desktop publishing skills, too.

Add summer camp or a cross-cultural ministry in your church, and you can tack another two pages onto this list. You'll handle situations and people that would make sociologists and psychologists call for backup.

And friend, that's just dealing with the kids. If you attend board meetings, you'd best also be a diplomat, accountant, and a business expert.

Plus, over half of your ministry isn't to children at all—it's to adults. You've got the kids' parents, the adults on your ministry staff, the volunteers, other folks on staff at the church, not to mention the level of leadership above you.

Feeling overloaded yet?

Many of us went into children's ministry because we wanted to spend all our time ministering to kids. That's not the reality of the situation. If you don't learn how to motivate and rally adults in ministry and how to train and delegate, you'll fail. You have to master those skills, too.

Effective leaders don't let themselves burn out doing everything themselves.

There's no way you can do everything yourself. You can try, but it won't work no matter how many hours you put in.

Here's the good news: You're not *supposed* to do everything yourself.

Read Ephesians 4:11-12 again. Remember: God gave some to be pastors and teachers, not so they could shoulder the entire Christian education program themselves, but so they could equip others for service.

Effective leaders don't let themselves burn out doing everything themselves. They help others become effective in doing ministry.

And that means you've got to stop doing it all yourself.

I see you nodding, but then sighing. "Brother Jim, you just don't understand. I've asked people to help me. I've *begged* people to help me. But these folks just won't do it. Since I'm the Christian education director, they think it's my job to make things happen."

Well, those folks are wrong. The Bible says so, and you should say so too.

"But Brother Jim, if I get everyone else doing ministry, what will *I* do? People will think they don't need me anymore."

Listen: You'll always have work to do. Leaders have plenty to keep themselves busy if they're leading the way God wants his people led.

Exodus 18:20-22 records some great advice Moses' father-in-law gave Moses about dealing with the people of Israel: "Teach them the decrees and laws, and show them the way to live and the duties they are to perform. But select capable men from all the people—men who fear God, trustworthy men who hate dishonest gain—and appoint them as officials over thousands, hundreds, fifties and tens."

You may not have thousands over which to appoint leadership yet, but I'll bet you've got ten. As a ministry leader, it's your job to find and equip those overseers and to shepherd them so they can shepherd others.

That's the job God has placed before you that only you can do. Others can set up chairs and hand out snacks at VBS. But only *you* can provide leadership to those who serve kids in your ministry.

So why are you spending all day typing up the kids' newsletter? Why are you straightening chairs after youth group? How come you're checking the battery in the wireless microphone? Couldn't someone else do it instead?

You can be so busy doing the work of the ministry that you don't get around to *doing* ministry. You don't pray. You don't work with your leaders. You don't do the follow-up and vision-casting that keeps your ministry moving forward.

Instead, you're running around looking for more crayons.

You must learn to delegate well. The alternative is ministry meltdown. Maybe not today or tomorrow, but someday. You're planting the seeds of your own destruction if you can't delegate. It's that important.

Delegation isn't a dirty word. It's not sloughing off your work or treating others badly. It's not giving away the crummy jobs and keeping the good stuff for yourself.

In Genesis 1:28, God blessed mankind and said, "Be fruitful and increase in number; fill the earth and subdue it. Rule over the fish of the sea and the birds of the air and over every living creature that moves on the ground." That's delegation. God gave us the skills and resources to rule over creation—to be caretakers—and then handed us the responsibility and authority to do the job.

When you delegate well, you give away not just a task or a responsibility but the *authority* to get the job done. Delegation can be fulfilling, not just for the person handing out the jobs but for the person who's been entrusted with a job.

Effective leaders delegate.

Here are nine steps to mastering delegation. Like most leadership skills, it begins not with how you do it—but with who you are.

1. Figure out why you're doing everything yourself.

Have a little chat with yourself and the Lord. Exactly why are you so overwhelmed? Answering that question tells you a lot about yourself and your ministry.

Perhaps it's because people expect too much of you. Get out your job description. Is it written anywhere, "Do everything that everybody expects, no matter how much and how long it takes?" If not, that means you can set reasonable boundaries.

Talk with your pastor. Point out everything on the job description you're expected to do and be honest about your struggles to get it all done. Ask for help deciding which things to quit doing.

Perhaps it's because you expect too much of yourself. If you've ever heard yourself say, "What would they do without me around here?" you're in trouble. The fact is that important people die every day, and the world doesn't screech to a halt. If you got hit by a truck this week, the Lord would find a way to get the important things done without you next week.

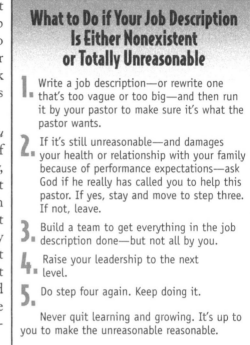

What to Do if Your Job Description Is Either Nonexistent or Totally Unreasonable

1. Write a job description—or rewrite one that's too vague or too big—and then run it by your pastor to make sure it's what the pastor wants.

2. If it's still unreasonable—and damages your health or relationship with your family because of performance expectations—ask God if he really has called you to help this pastor. If yes, stay and move to step three. If not, leave.

3. Build a team to get everything in the job description done—but not all by you.

4. Raise your leadership to the next level.

5. Do step four again. Keep doing it.

Never quit learning and growing. It's up to you to make the unreasonable reasonable.

If you're trying to earn the Lord's favor, or peoples' favor, by being a workaholic, repent now. If you can't feel good about yourself unless the Christmas pageant goes off without a hitch, lighten up. The wings always fall off an angel, or the donkey wanders off down the aisle, or Mary drops the baby Jesus doll. People expect it. They even *enjoy* it.

My point: You're not perfect. The Lord knows it, people know it, so it's important you realize that nobody expects it. Nobody but you, that is.

Perhaps you think nobody can do things quite as well as you can. You're probably right. When you delegate a task, sometimes the quality slips a bit. You can overcome that by providing good training, but even then the person who leads singing may not do it as well as you can…at first.

But how did you develop your skills? Probably because someone let you sorry all over a bunch of kids until you got better at leading.

Do this for me—and for yourself: Make sure the problem isn't your pride. I've known ministry workers who take so much ownership of their ideas or programs that they can't turn their babies over to others. These folks refuse to delegate. They're like jealous parents, and they drive away the help they need.

Perhaps you're running ahead of God's timing. You believe God wants you to launch an after-school tutoring program to reach hundreds of elementary latchkey kids. But you can't get enough adults to the building by 3:30 each day to get the program off the ground.

Consider: Maybe it's time to start small, and let God bring the resources you need to implement your larger vision.

If you're doing everything yourself, your first task is to fix that situation. Why? Because when you leave, the wheels will fall off the ministry. You'll have failed to leave a successor.

2. Identify and develop the skills you need to delegate effectively.

You can't delegate a job you can't define, so you'd better learn to write job descriptions (p. 103). People aren't going to take on jobs until they understand the scope of what you're asking them to do.

And while you're at it, you'd better master the technology available to you.

I remember my first computer. People told me it would save me time and help organize our ministry, but for the first few days I sure couldn't see it. All I did was type. I didn't talk to people, make visits, or write lessons. I built databases.

"Great," I thought, "I'm further behind now than I've *ever* been."

But then I hit the "sort" button and stuff that had been impossible to find appeared in alphabetical order. I could delegate tasks because at last I could give people the information they needed to be successful.

If you find yourself saying, "It's easier for me to do it myself" because you don't know how to put together a spreadsheet, *learn to put together spreadsheets.* Someone in your church can show you.

Don't let a lack of skills (budgeting, planning, recruiting, whatever) get in the way of being able to delegate tasks. It's worth learning what you need to learn—you'll recover your investment of time many times over.

3. Get good at what you do so you can train others.

A confession: I'm not the best possible person to be doing everything in my job description. For instance, I'm not the guy you want laying out our publications or tracking down all the articles we print. But I can do it well enough to explain to a graphics person and a writer what needs doing—and why.

You don't need to be an expert children's bell choir director to delegate the task of directing the bell choir. But you do need to be able to communicate what that bell choir director should accomplish and provide the resources and leadership that director needs to be successful.

Remember: You can't delegate to people who aren't following you. You earn the option of delegating when you earn the respect of your followers.

4. Be ready to delegate.

You want to know why the Lord won't send one hundred volunteers to you next week, each one wanting to help out in your ministry? Maybe it's because if they did come, you wouldn't be able to put them to work.

Until you know what you'll do with volunteers—which jobs they'll get, how they'll be trained, and when they'll start—don't expect God to send them to you.

Be ready to qualify volunteers God sends, identifying their gifts. Not everyone who wants to help you can do so. Some people are just not cut out to work in children's or youth ministry.

If someone thinks kids should be seen and not heard, that's not a hot candidate. Neither is someone who just wants to play games and who describes himself as a "big kid."

The world is full of people who are loving and sweet, but they simply have no business being with kids or youth. They lack the aptitudes or gifts. No amount of study will overcome a teacher's inability to put up with wiggles and giggles down in the preschool room. If God designed someone to require order and quiet with a place for everything and everything in its place, children's ministry is not for that person.

So don't place those people in your ministry and delegate responsibility to them. It's better to have *no* volunteers than the wrong volunteers.

How do you determine a person's giftedness? There are plenty of surveys and tests available, but I've found that gifts tend to track along with what people do well, enjoy doing, and find fulfilling. So long as those things glorify God and build up the church, I suspect they're working within their spiritual giftedness. And the way to confirm that is to actually get folks into appropriate areas of service, and see how they take to it.

5. Equip others to help you.

Even when God sends the right people, you've got to train them before you can delegate tasks to them.

Be wise about training. Pour yourself into increasing the skills of the people on your team, but do it in the right way.

Training isn't verbal. It's *modeling*. It's letting a learner come alongside someone who already knows how to do it. There's time to watch, time to ask questions, time to try things and get immediate, informed feedback.

If you think training is just a matter of tossing a book at new teachers or having them sit through a few classes, may the Lord save your students. And your teachers. It's not going to be a pretty sight.

You cannot successfully delegate tasks to people who are unprepared to receive them. That's like having a football quarterback toss the ball downfield to the team mascot instead of a receiver. It's just not going to work.

What's your training program look like? If it's not the admiration of your ministry buddies, make it that way. And making it that way is as easy as asking your very best teachers to mentor new teachers. Creating a master-teacher level of volunteers not only works in public schools, it also works in Christian education.

6. Delegate and then release.

Start by getting people trained, then delegating an assignment consistent with each volunteer's gifting. Then allow volunteers to do ministry—in their own unique ways.

You've got to do two things at the same time: Make a delegated job incredibly simple but not boring.

Here's what I mean...

Suppose you've got a music leader in a children's assembly. You'll want to make sure she's good with children and understands how to worship. You'll want to make sure she selects songs that fit your program and your kids. There's a lot you'll want to spell out so what she does blesses the children.

But you've also got to let her have some room to express herself. Nobody wants to volunteer for a job that's so structured it's boring. If she's going to grow in that role, there's got to be room for her to grow.

And another thing: You've got to be willing to delegate some of the fun jobs you'd rather do yourself. I happen to love leading music in kids' church, but I've got to be a big enough leader to let someone else take that role.

Is there a job you've hung onto that someone else could do? If you delegated that job, what could you do with the time and energy it freed up?

7. Evaluate.

When you delegate a task, that doesn't mean you're done with it forever. You've got to follow up and check on the outcome.

People won't always tell you if they need more training or if the task isn't going well. They may not even know they're in trouble until it's too late. If it's the first time they've ever done the job, they miss the danger signs.

Go inspect. Make midcourse corrections. Encourage. Empower. Confront. Find out if there are problems and fix them.

8. Keep communicating your vision.

The people who have already responded to you and your vision, and to whom you've already delegated tasks, still need to hear from you.

In fact, they may need to hear from you *more* than the people who haven't yet responded to your invitation to come do ministry with kids. Now that they've taught classes or stuffed envelopes or poured lemonade awhile, the shine may have worn off the job.

We sometimes forget about the "old faithful" who've worked alongside us forever. And man, that's an expensive mistake.

You want to keep those precious people on board, so keep the vision in front of them. Coach them. Ask them if they're ready to handle more responsibility or if they want to move to another job that serves the Lord and helps reach the vision for your ministry.

9. Give credit where credit is due.

If you delegated preparing last week's flier to Sarah, and your pastor compliments you on the design, pass that compliment along to Sarah. And make sure your pastor knows it was her work. Ask your pastor to thank her personally.

Become a cheerleader for your team, and you'll find that other people want to join the team. It's just natural.

And give credit to God, too. Don't think for a moment that growth in your ministry is only due to you. It's all about you following God's plan, and God using you.

Get a reputation for humility. For sharing the glory. For integrity. Earn a reputation like that, and you'll find people far more willing to take on tasks you want to delegate.

And keep in mind that the more skills you build as a leader, the better you'll be able to delegate. The next few chapters will help you master the use of key leadership skills so you can add them to your "leaders toolbox."

10. Problem Solving

Want to test the measure of a leader? Throw a problem at him or her.

When most people come face to face with problems, they immediately look for others to solve them.

We all start out that way. As children, when problems came our way, we called for our mamas. And that was completely appropriate for a child—but not for a leader. It's a follower mentality.

Leaders respond differently when facing a problem. They act to solve it.

Those sorts of people are like Daniel.

Here's how Daniel is described in Daniel 5:12: "This man Daniel, whom the king called Belteshazzar, was found to have a keen mind and knowledge and understanding, and also the ability to interpret dreams, explain riddles and solve difficult problems."

Daniel had a reputation for being able to solve problems. It's a reputation you want to earn too.

But before we talk about how to solve problems, there are a couple things you need to know about problems…

Not all problems are bad.

I often hear ministry workers wish they lived problem-free lives.

Well, there are people who have a problem-free existence, but they're all dead. The only people I know who don't have to deal with challenges like stress, budgets, and relationships are stretched out in the cemetery.

Notice I said *challenges* rather than *problems*. That's no accident. I've found that some things I considered problems turned out to be tremendous blessings. They're the very situations that helped me grow and changed my life for the better.

Whatever problems you face in ministry, decide to view them not just as problems but also as challenges God wants to help guide you through. That attitude keeps you teachable—and invites God's guidance.

You may look back at the problems in your life right now, and thank God for them because they caused you to grow. And here's why…

Some problems prepare you to handle more.

Problems season you and prepare you for more responsibility.

When David walked out to face Goliath, it wasn't the first time he'd fought a larger enemy. He'd already bested a lion and a bear. Goliath might be carrying a spear, but David knew he could place a rock in just the right place to drop the giant. David had faced down big, hairy problems before.

Think about your life. How many of the problems you've faced were just training? Warm-ups that prepared you for larger problems that followed?

Some problems are learning opportunities.

I remember the day we decided to start a puppet ministry at my church. I'd never held a puppet before, but my roommate was on a college puppet team.

My friend walked us through what we needed to know. And I took *really* good notes because the next week I was going to be in charge. From absolute ignoramus to mister director in one week—quite a transformation. But that ministry was successful.

If I'd seen my lack of experience as a problem, it would have stopped me cold. Instead, I saw it as a challenge, and in the process of overcoming it, I learned a new skill.

What current challenges are teaching you something new?

Like it or not, you've *got* to be a problem solver.

People who serve under you already see you as a problem solver—and they need you to take on that role.

For most of us in children's ministry, problem solving isn't our strongest skill. We're wired to be caretakers. We love feeding the sheep God's entrusted to us. We're natural born teachers.

We're *not* so good at doing the administrative analysis, measuring, and evaluation that help us solve problems *before* they develop into full-blown crises.

Does the notion that people expect you to solve problems make you uncomfortable? If so, you're in good company. There's a long list of outstanding leaders in Scripture who failed as problem solvers.

When the people told Moses they needed water, Moses smacked a rock with a stick—which disappointed God. Daniel fell short now and then in the problem-solving department. Peter wanted to do something to help out Jesus in the Garden, so he drew a sword and lopped off someone's ear.

Being a problem solver doesn't mean you always have the right answer at your fingertips. Or that you always make the right decision or do the right thing. But it does mean you're willing to make decisions and face problems head on.

Do you think of yourself as a problem solver?

I've watched excellent problem solvers, and here are some characteristics they display when it's time to toss rocks at their Goliaths.

Problem-Solver Characteristics

PROBLEM SOLVERS ARE WILLING TO GIVE IT A TRY.

If you walk past a fence that needs to be painted often enough, you'll quit noticing that the paint is peeling. You get used to the problem. And when you get used to problems, they quit feeling like problems. You no longer feel an urgency to roll up your sleeves and try to fix things.

Leaders identify challenges as challenges—and they act. *They think of themselves as problem solvers.* They're proactive and intentional in making things better.

What's your approach when a challenge finds you? Do you turn and face it? Or do you ignore it, hoping it'll go away?

PROBLEM SOLVERS EXPLORE OPTIONS.

A friend of mine calls now and then, and he always says, "I think God's calling me to leave this church and go to another church." Then he lists all the challenges he's currently facing.

So I ask, "Why don't you get out of there? If God's calling you somewhere else, quit so you're ready to move forward."

That's when he backpedals. "Well, then I'd just be facing a whole new set of problems. At least here I know what they are."

He's right: He will find new challenges wherever he goes—that's life. But if God's calling him to move, God will help him deal with the challenges he runs into down the road. My friend just isn't willing to explore new opportunities. He's stuck.

We get stuck too. Maybe it's fear or apathy or just being worn out, but sometimes when our first try to solve a problem doesn't work, we surrender.

But the first solution often isn't the best solution. Best solutions are often the third…or fourth…or twentieth idea that comes to mind when you're figuring out how to get through or around a challenge.

How quickly do you stop at your first solution? How well do you explore options?

PROBLEM SOLVERS SEEK THE ADVICE OF OTHERS.

I remember trying to put a swing set together for my daughters. The instructions made no sense to me, so I found someone who'd put a swing set together for his kids. He told me he'd made a complete mess of the entire thing.

That's the guy I asked to come on over. As he described what he'd done I did the opposite—and the project came together.

Effective problem solvers don't necessarily look for advice from the smartest person they know. They look for someone who's tackled the problem. Even if that person failed, you can learn something.

And notice that good problem solvers aren't afraid to ask for advice. They're open to new information. They're willing to admit that they don't have all the answers.

Will you admit it when you don't know—and ask for advice?

PROBLEM SOLVERS TAKE REASONABLE RISKS.

There are risks involved in everything. But there are risks, and there are *risks*. Not every risk is worth taking.

Reasonable risks include things that don't jeopardize your health or the lives of people you serve. They don't create total chaos and confusion in your ministry. They don't have people questioning your salvation or your sanity.

But they *do* include trying new things, stretching yourself.

And if God clearly tells you to do something, that's no risk at all—no matter how strange it might sound. When God told Noah to take up boat building, it had to sound like the craziest thing anyone had ever heard…until the rain started to fall.

You'll never step out and be the leader God wants you to be without taking risks. Are you willing?

PROBLEM SOLVERS PRAY.

I know people who frantically try one solution after another when they hit a problem, and when all else fails, they pray.

That's backward.

Listen, if you're leading in the church, you need to be a person of prayer. If you lead by your sight alone, you're headed for a cliff—and you're leading everyone right along with you.

Pray about decisions and challenges *first*. Allow God to guide and use you. That's what he wants…and that's who you're working for.

Ten Strategies for Solving Problems

As I've watched leaders I admire face challenges, I've taken notes. And over the years I've put together a twelve-step process that's served me well when challenges come my way. I'd suggest you use it too.

1. Listen for God's answer.

Now and then, when I've gone to the Lord about a problem, he's clearly shown me what to do. So I did exactly what he said, and the problem was solved. "Thus sayeth the Lord" always works.

But many times the Lord doesn't provide me with a clear answer. Maybe I'm not listening, but there are times I ask for guidance and hear…nothing. And the problem is still sitting there.

> **When problems present themselves, do you pray?**

Personally, I think the Lord doesn't care how you solve some problems, so long as your solution honors him. He leaves it up to you. He just wants you to solve the problem. He's given you permission.

When problems present themselves, do you pray? And do you listen for God's answer?

2. Identify the problem clearly.

When you face a challenge, figure out precisely what problem you're trying to solve. And I mean *precisely*. Get it down to one sentence that everyone involved can agree on. Otherwise, you'll spend a lot of time fixing the wrong stuff.

The other day as I walked down the hall between services at our church I saw a weeping woman standing by our elementary registration table. A *pregnant* weeping woman. A pregnant weeping woman holding a *form*.

The lady was sobbing, but what was the problem? Was it related to the people at the registration table? Or was it a health difficulty related to her pregnancy? Had something happened during our ministry time that got her crying? Was there a problem with the form? Was her crying a good thing or a bad thing? Before I could help provide a solution, I had to figure out what was going on over there. I had absolutely no idea.

It turned out she'd been handed a preschool form by accident, and the volunteers couldn't find the right elementary form to replace it. That's all. No big spiritual crisis.

The next day I realized the root issue wasn't the woman: We seldom get people breaking into tears at the registration table. But we did give out the wrong forms. There were fourteen separate steps in fixing what went wrong, from initiating new policies and procedures (when you're at the table and run out of forms, who do you tell?) to keeping additional forms in a more assessable place (locking them in the church office wasn't the best idea) to having a box of tissues convenient.

When you're faced with a challenge, do you take the time to make certain you know exactly what it is—before you try to solve it?

3. Ask "Why did this happen?"

It's not enough to identify a problem and find a solution for it. That's good, but you need to take it a step further. You've got to then discover *why* the problem happened.

I was out of town once when I got a message that the overhead door in our children's ministry area had come off the hinges. A repair company was fixing it. The problem was under control.

Well, almost. Why—in the middle of the week when nobody was using that room—did the door come unhinged?

It turned out that someone who was giving a tour of the facility didn't know how to operate the controls. Which meant if we left the key that operated the garage-door motor in the box with other keys, this could happen again during the next tour.

Fixing the door was just *part* of the problem.

The good news is that there are plenty of problems and challenges to keep you busy. You don't have to face the same ones over and over. In fact, if that's happening, *you're* most likely the problem.

How faithful are you at digging to find out why a problem happened?

4. List ways to solve the problem.

Almost always there are many ways to solve any one problem. Some are good, some are bad, but they're all possibilities. And you want to see them all before you throw any of them away.

Choose the best, realizing that what's best today may change tomorrow.

At a church where I served, some very smart people decided the best way to provide music in the sanctuary was to install a pipe organ. It cost a fortune. Later, when sound systems came along, their decision didn't seem so smart— times had changed.

Don't get caught in the trap of thinking your best solutions for problems will *always* be best. Stay open to making up new lists of possibilities frequently.

Is your way always the best way? Is the first solution you tumble across the one you usually select? Are you open to changing that?

5. Identify factors that limit what decision you can make.

Maybe the best possible solution to your ongoing transportation problem is for your church to buy a fleet of buses. But with $18.74 in the church savings account, it's too expensive.

Cost is often a limiting factor. So is effort. And church political considerations are always something to keep in mind.

It may come as a shock, but politics can creep in even at church. Maybe the week after your VBS crafts destroyed the carpet isn't the time to ask for new computers. Timing can be everything.

What are the factors that matter in your church? Are they cost, effort, politics, timing, or other things? You'd better know because, like it or not, those factors determine in part how you go about solving problems.

6. Remember to consult history.

How has the problem been handled in the past? If you can keep from making the same mistake your predecessor made, good for you. Ask some longtime volunteers what's been done before. Don't reinvent the wheel.

And check around outside your own church for insights, too.

A few years ago we decided to give our bus workers one Saturday a month off. Seemed OK to us, but we'd never tried it. We had no idea what it would do to our program.

So I got on the phone and called around. I never did find a church who did that precise thing, but a church in New York gave its workers the entire summer off. So I peppered its staff members with questions: How did it affect the program? How eager were the workers to come back? How did it impact the kids? I learned from their history.

7. Determine if this solution is an exception or sets a precedent.

Once you give the OK once, you may set yourself up for making this the solution you always have to provide.

Suppose you absolutely cannot find volunteer nursery workers for a special service. So you call up some high school girls and one nursery supervisor and offer to pay them to cover the nursery.

Have you just set the expectation that during all special meetings you'll pay people to help? Unless you're clear this was a one-time exception, you've set a precedent you'll need to live with forever.

8. Ask yourself: Do you feel good about your proposed solution?

Does your solution have integrity? Will you be proud to raise your hand when someone asks where it came from?

It's tempting to shave corners or to take an easy way out to avoid conflict. But if you're considering a solution that doesn't maintain the highest standard of integrity, God won't let you feel peace about it. Listen to God's voice and obey the prompting.

9. Consider your solution from another person's perspective.

Sometimes solving one problem creates other problems. And solving a problem in a way that makes sense to one person may confuse everyone else.

For instance, in an effort to be seeker sensitive you might post some "Seeker Parking Only" signs in the parking lot next to your building.

And for two Sundays nobody parks there. Nobody. Senior citizens who appreciated parking close to the door are upset. Moms who lug in babies, diaper bags, and who knows what else are upset. And your visitors—who don't know what *seeker* means—are still hiking in from the far side of the lot.

Listen to God's voice and obey the prompting.

As a last step before implementing a problem-solving solution ask: How will it appear to others? Does your solution cause more problems than it solves?

10. Put feet under your plan—then evaluate.

Once you've planned the work, work your plan, and see how it goes. You'll discover wrinkles you couldn't anticipate until you actually rolled it out. Don't be disappointed when they appear; it's part of the process. Fix them.

Then ask: Were you successful? Are you seeing the results you wanted? Don't skip this step—it's the payoff! And it's where you see if it's time to start over.

Don'ts and Do's in Problem Solving

DON'T BE AFRAID TO SAY, "I DON'T KNOW," "I'LL LOOK INTO IT," OR "I'LL GET BACK TO YOU."

There are times you don't have all the facts. Or you need to check with your pastor. Or you simply aren't ready to make a decision. When you're in any of those spots, refuse to make a decision until you do your homework.

Just make sure that if you promise to get back to someone, you do so in a timely fashion.

DON'T BE RUSHED.

Don't let yourself be pressured into making a decision too quickly.

In hospital emergency rooms, not all problems are equal. Limp in with a sore toe, and you'll get bumped back behind someone who arrives on two separate stretchers.

The process is called *triage*, which is a fancy medical word for "deciding who needs help now, who can wait, and who's past help." Do triage with your Christian education program.

I walk down the hall at our church and I can see twenty-eight things that need improving. I'd be a very frustrated man if I couldn't also see that twenty-six of those things aren't critical—they can wait. I really only have to get two of the things on my list fixed in the next week.

DON'T IGNORE TRENDS.

I'm a fanatic about checking attendance numbers from week to week. Not just totals, but by age group and class. I chart and compare numbers constantly.

I'm looking for developing trends in attendance and budgeting. I know where we hit walls last year; I want to know if we're hitting the same walls again.

You see, if you're addressing the same problems you've addressed before, what you think is the problem isn't *really* the problem. Either you've fixed the wrong thing or else you're just really bad at fixing that problem.

If every June you run out of money, you're not doing the right things with the information you've received. You've missed a predictable trend.

DON'T WAIT FOR PROBLEMS TO MANIFEST THEMSELVES TO FIX THEM.

Look ahead. Ask yourself, "If we grow by 20 percent this year, how will our Sunday school classrooms work?" If you know that you'll need to make a change then, make that change now. You'll be ahead of the curve and ready for growth.

The perfect time to fix something is *before* it breaks.

And it's worth your time to develop a "Plan B" for situations that call for decisions. What if it rains? if the power goes out? if nobody shows up?

DON'T FOCUS ON THE PROBLEM ONCE YOU'VE GOT A SOLUTION. FOCUS ON THE SOLUTION.

The Apostle Peter stepped out of a boat to walk on water to where Jesus stood. Bold move, especially for a fisherman who was familiar with the sea.

Peter didn't need to worry about waves. The solution for his buoyancy problem was right in front of him: Jesus. But Peter couldn't quite stop focusing on the waves; he took his eyes off Jesus, and that sunk him in a hurry.

We can learn something from Peter. When we've got a solution in sight, let's stay focused on it, not on the problem. As hard as it is to let go of the problem, it's essential. Otherwise we don't put our wholehearted energy into making the solution work.

And if the solution is forgiving someone, do it and move on. I know people who still talk about problems they solved twenty years ago. That's when a conflict flared up, was worked through, and forgiven…but someone still remembers and still brings it up. That's not healthy. Or Christian.

DON'T KEEP DOING WHAT CAUSED THE PROBLEM IN THE FIRST PLACE.

My wife turned to me the other day and said, "I want to learn to use a computer."

I couldn't believe it. I'd bought lots of computers, but she had never wanted to even try using them.

But Julie had realized that if our home-based business is going to increase, more than one person needs to be able to do the work. And all the work is done on computer.

Julie understood that if we always do what we've always done, we'll always have what we've always had. Period. It's a law of nature, like gravity. The only way to break free and see new results is to make changes.

Something in your church or ministry allowed a problem to develop. Don't keep doing whatever it was that gave that problem the chance to form. Make changes.

DON'T SOLVE EVERYONE'S PROBLEMS FOR THEM.

Leaders sometimes step in too quickly to solve problems. The person experiencing the problem doesn't get a chance to learn by fixing it.

If you want people who are serving with you in ministry to grow, ask them what they think they should do with a problem they bring to you. Give them the chance to solve it.

DON'T FALL IN LOVE WITH YOUR PAST SUCCESSES.

OK, the idea worked in a church you used to serve. But what worked there may not work here. Be open to new ideas and approaches. The problem you face may only feel familiar; old solutions probably won't work.

DON'T EVER FORGET: JESUS LIVES INSIDE YOU.

If God placed you in charge of a ministry or bus route or classroom or section of the parking lot, that's not an accident.

God is for you. No matter how tough your situation may be, remember God loves you and wants you to be successful in providing leadership.

You're not powerless. Your work is not wasted. You're not alone.

Did I make my point?

The most important thing you can do with a problem is also the one thing that may frighten you most: Confront it head on. Don't ignore it. Don't hope it'll go away or get better on its own.

You're a leader and that means you're a problem solver.

If now isn't the time to tackle the problem, when will be a better time?

See the next page for the top ten do's in effective problem solving.

The Top Ten Do's in Problem Solving

10. Do solve the problem—don't run from it.

9. Do solve the problem—don't run from it.

8. Do solve the problem—don't run from it.

7. Do solve the problem—don't run from it.

6. Do solve the problem—don't run from it.

5. Do solve the problem—don't run from it.

4. Do solve the problem—don't run from it.

3. Do solve the problem—don't run from it.

2. Do solve the problem—don't run from it.

1. Do solve the problem—don't run from it.

11. Making Difficult Decisions

Here's the good news: God created us with the ability to make decisions.

And here's the bad news: God created us with the ability to make decisions.

As a leader you'll make lots of decisions. It's the ability to make difficult decisions that sets leaders apart from followers.

The most important decision comes first.

Let me remind you of a familiar passage about making decisions.

In the book of Joshua, Chapters 23 and 24, we get to see a remarkable leader in action. Joshua gathered God's people together and reminded them of all God had done to deliver them from their enemies—and from themselves.

Then Joshua brought the history lesson down to a clear decision: "But if serving the Lord seems undesirable to you, then choose for yourselves this day whom you will serve...But as for me and my household, we will serve the Lord" (Joshua 24:15).

Joshua knew each person listening could choose to serve. But no matter what anyone else did, Joshua intended to make the right choice. And when Israel's leader chose to follow God, that allowed God to let blessings flow through Joshua to the people who followed Joshua.

Joshua knew something that maybe you're just figuring out: The higher up in leadership you are, the tougher the decisions you'll face...and the more people will be affected by your decisions.

Fortunately, most of the decisions I made as a teenager affected only me. When I made mistakes, I paid the price, dusted myself off, and moved on.

But when I got older and became a husband and father, my decisions affected not only me but also my wife and children. The impact of decisions I made had far greater consequences.

And when I became a pastor, suddenly my decisions affected not just me, not just my family, but hundreds of families. Thousands of people.

We all make poor decisions. What we do, how we act, what we say; there are plenty of opportunities to make bad calls. I know I've made my share.

At my first church, I led a kids' ministry without once thinking like a parent when I scheduled meetings and activities. I'm lucky those parents didn't hurt me. I made some horrible choices. If any of those parents are reading this, please accept my apology right here and now.

Decisions matter. Leaders win or lose based on how they choose.

The first and most difficult decision you face is deciding whether you'll do things your way or listen to the Lord and do things his way. Joshua made that decision, and it set the tone for the rest of his decisions.

I hear you: *Of course*, you'll do things God's way. You're a ministry leader, right?

But what about when you're thinking it's time for you to move to a new ministry because you just can't seem to get things in gear where you are? What about giving up old techniques and trying something new? What about choosing to live a life that wouldn't shame you if everyone knew your business?

I remember when I played for a Christian band and we were right on the edge of landing a record contract. That came at the same time I was also offered a full-time job doing ministry at a church—for fifty bucks a week.

That's right. Full time, a whopping fifty bucks a week. I was making more than that in the *band*.

But after prayer I knew what God wanted for me—so I went to the church.

The proof of a good decision isn't how you feel about the decision. The proof is fruit that comes from your decision. Is your ministry bearing more fruit because you decided to add a bus route or picked a new person to lead your preschool room? Every decision brings good fruit…or not.

"I want your decision…now."

Some decisions demand immediate attention. When a child is physically hurt in your classroom, you've got to act—now. But there are other decisions that can and should wait.

Effective leaders don't always make quick decisions. If your facility is on fire, then a quick decision is called for. But unless flames are licking at your feet, you can probably take time to make a deliberate decision. It's best to delay if…

- **You're tired.** When I'm tired, I just can't get excited about anything. Everything seems like a bad idea. If you're the same when you're overwhelmed or exhausted, it's smart to say, "Let me get back to you on that."

- **You don't have enough information.** If a little alarm goes off in your head that maybe you'd better check with the pastor, church treasurer, the head custodian, or someone else whose opinion will make a difference, don't make a decision yet. Make a few calls first.

- **You haven't heard from all the right people.** The toughest decisions often involve managing people. Should you fire someone? (See page 101.) Dive in and help two other leaders resolve conflict? Before you make an uninformed decision, let everyone who needs to weigh in do so.

Now, some people procrastinate when it comes to making tough decisions. It's as if they're waiting for Jesus to come back so they don't have to make the hard call at all. That doesn't work—you've *got* to make decisions.

Remember: *Leaders are decision makers.* And leaders take the responsibility for their decisions.

Taking Responsibility for Decisions

Many people make decisions, but not all those people will take responsibility for their decisions. And a willingness to make decisions and then own them is the difference between leaders and followers.

Followers blame others. It's always somebody else's fault or some unavoidable situation that arose. Followers make excuses. Leaders don't. Leaders know the truth of this statement: *You can't explain your way out of something you behaved yourself into.*

If you said you'd line up nursery workers and you didn't, don't make excuses. If you failed to prepare your Bible lesson and you let down the kids, don't explain how work went crazy and that kept you from preparing.

There may be valid reasons you couldn't follow through. Things do come up; that's life. But if you let those things become excuses, that's a follower mentality.

Leaders take responsibility for what they decide—and what they do.

There's a guy on my staff I really respect. When I correct him, he never makes excuses. He listens, makes sure he understands, and then says, "That mistake will never happen again."

And it doesn't. Instead, he pushes ahead and makes a different mistake—which is fine by me. That's what I'm after. If you're not making mistakes, you're not trying anything new. Make all the new mistakes you want—but take responsibility for them.

Why Leaders Make Poor Decisions

Here are six of the most common traps. Are you falling into any of them?

Trap 1: They succumb to fear.

In Matthew 25:14-30 we read a parable Jesus told about three servants who received talents from their boss. One got five talents, the next guy got two, and the third man got one talent.

You know the story. The first and second guys did something with the money they received, and both of them earned a "well done" from their master.

In verse 18 we see the third man bury the money. Why? The answer is there in verses 24 and 25, "I knew that you are a hard man...So I was *afraid* [italics added]."

We almost always make poor decisions when we let fear guide us.

Trap 2: They rely on their own abilities and wisdom.

We all bring some experience to our leadership. We've developed abilities and accumulated some wisdom, and that's a plus.

But it can also be a weakness.

You can get in trouble if you're trying to lead under your own steam. If all you've got going for you is what you bring to the task, you're in trouble.

Proverbs 3:5-8 says, "Trust in the Lord with all your heart and lean not on your own understanding; in all your ways acknowledge him, and he will make your paths straight. Do not be wise in your own eyes; fear the Lord and shun evil. This will bring health to your body and nourishment to your bones."

Now, nobody needs to tell me I don't know it all. I first came to the Lord because I nearly killed myself so often during my first seventeen years that I knew I needed a Savior. Nobody needed to convince me I'd made a mess of things. Leaning on my own understanding wasn't getting me anywhere.

If you want to make right decisions, lean on God's strength and wisdom. Before you make a decision, ask yourself: What does God say about it?

Proverbs 14:12 says, "There is a way that seems right to a man, but in the end it leads to death." There are a lot of things that seem right to us— but aren't right. Our wisdom is limited; we can get things wrong even with good intentions.

If I'm relying on myself alone, I'm going to make poor decisions. I know it may sound trite, but I've got to ask you: How much time do you spend in prayer about decisions you're facing? Are you asking God for the wisdom you need?

TRAP 3: They let emotions and feelings cloud their judgment.

When I was young, my strategy for conflict resolution was to get in the first lick. I'd come up to you, pick up a chair, and smack you up side the head. I'd hit you one time, hard and ferocious. That pretty well settled it.

But when I became a Christian, someone pointed out I couldn't do that anymore. I had to talk about things and settle the conflict with words.

That was a hard transition. My emotions said, "Pick up a chair and let it fly," but I knew better. So sometimes I'd stop the discussion and ask if I could get back to the person I was fighting with. I needed to calm down.

It's hard to make a good decision when you're wrapped up in your emotions. Second Corinthians 5:7 says, "We live by faith, not by sight."

It's not what we think. Or feel. Or wish. It's what God says. That's where the good decisions are. If we make decisions based on our emotions, we're basing our decisions on the wrong thing.

TRAP 4: They let themselves be pressured into making decisions.

Just because you're standing in my office wanting a decision doesn't mean I'll give you one. Especially if I don't *have* an answer.

Pressure can sap your energy and siphon off your joy.

It's tempting to tell people something just so they'll go away. But that's a great way to say something stupid that you'll have to live with.

Pressure closes down your thinking. Narrows your options. Pile on enough pressure, and it'll literally kill you. And pressure most certainly increases the likelihood that your decisions will be poor ones.

What causes pressure in your life? Is it a church board that's demanding results? an out-of-control schedule? Is it your attempt to double attendance—even if nobody else expects it? Pressure can sap your energy and siphon off your joy.

And by the way—the source of that pressure will never be the Lord.

"Come to me, all you who are weary and burdened, and I will give you rest. Take my yoke upon you and learn from me, for I am gentle and humble in heart, and you will find rest for your souls. For my yoke is easy and my burden is light" (Matthew 11:28-30) says it all. You have plenty to do—but you don't have to do it alone. When you work for God, you won't be overwhelmed.

TRAP 5: They do what others do rather than what God has called them to do.

"Thus sayeth the Lord" always works. Underline that. Highlight it. Copy it down, and hang it on your bulletin board. Write it on your planning calendar. Those six words will give you success in ministry like nothing else.

Maybe it's crazy for me to say this, since I do seminars all over the country, but it's true: Nowhere in the Bible does it say that you should do as the seminar speaker does. What works for us at Church on the Move may be the worst possible thing for you to do at your church.

Write down all the speaker's ideas, and learn from his or her experience. But when you get home put those notes in a drawer. Before you do anything you wrote down, ask God what you should do in *your* local church. What does he want to do through *you*? Once you've got that straight, pull out the notes, and see if anything you wrote down will help you get there.

"Thus sayeth the Lord" *always* works.

TRAP 6: They don't really trust God.

There's a difference between knowing who God is and trusting him.

Here's what Psalm 37:3-6 says: "Trust in the Lord and do good; dwell in the land and enjoy safe pasture. Delight yourself in the Lord and he will give you the desires of your heart. Commit your way to the Lord; trust in him and he will do this: He will make your righteousness shine like the dawn, the justice of your cause like the noonday sun."

When you put your trust in the Lord, you act on what the Word of God says. If Scripture weighs in on a decision you need to make, take God at his word and do what he says.

When we ignore God's Word, we make poor decisions.

Keys to Making Good Decisions

I've yet to meet someone who launched a string of disasters on purpose.

But how do you avoid it? When you consider all the things that can go wrong, it's amazing any good decisions get made at all!

Here's my advice on making good decisions…

DECIDE YOU'LL MAKE THE *BEST* DECISION.

When you're faced with making a decision, almost always a solution will immediately spring to mind. That solution usually involves your doing what you've always done. But is it the best answer?

We're creatures of habit in church work. If something worked well once, we stick with it until something goes wrong or the Lord comes back.

When Julie and I first got married, I did the cooking throughout the week and she fixed Sunday dinner. And that first Sunday we had meatloaf. Not just meatloaf—a *great* meatloaf. I loved it. It was about as good as a meatloaf gets.

The second Sunday there it was again: meatloaf. Why mess with a good thing, right? Except even a great meatloaf is still a meatloaf. I asked if maybe the next Sunday we could do something different, and Julie agreed.

The third Sunday we had meatloaf *balls*. Little individual meatloaves. And the fourth Sunday we were back to meatloaf.

I finally asked Julie if she could cook anything else. She couldn't. "But I make meatloaf really well, don't I?" she asked.

I'm happy to report that her cooking skills have widened remarkably (and so has her husband), and now when meatloaf appears, I'm happy to see it. If you ever come over to my house to eat, call ahead and ask her to make it—see if it isn't the best meatloaf you've ever tasted.

But that's how it is for us in church work, too: We have success once with a program, so we keep going back to it. We don't ask the hard question: Is this the *best* thing we could do with this time, money, and energy?

When it's time once again to run a program you've done before, do this: Ask your pastor, "I know we've always done it this way, but is there any reason you'd like to see it done differently?" Or grab a couple of your best people, put them in a room and ask, "If we couldn't do it the way we've always done it, what would you do?"

CONSIDER THE TIMING.

Is this the best time to implement your decision?

Can you dedicate sufficient time to see that what's necessary for success gets done? Would this interfere with another important initiative that's already underway? Will this step on toes you can miss if you wait a week?

Making a good decision is just part of the deal. You've also got to implement it. And timing is everything when it comes to that.

Here's a nugget that cost me dearly to learn: *Making a great decision doesn't mean much if you present it poorly or at the wrong time.*

There are times I've been certain I heard from the Lord on an issue. I knew in my bones the answer I had was the best possible one. But because I presented it poorly—or at the wrong time—it wasn't considered as a solution.

Maybe you work for someone who needs to see graphs, charts, and timelines before giving the OK to move ahead. Fine—make graphs, charts, and timelines. Or maybe you work for someone who has to think it was his or her idea before giving it serious consideration. Fine—let your boss think that it was his or her idea.

Or maybe the answer will be received better if it's presented by someone else. If necessary, give the idea away, and let someone else get credit. It doesn't matter as long as your ministry moves forward. The important thing is that you heard God's direction, and it got accomplished.

When you ask God for guidance in selecting the best answer, also ask for wisdom in how and when to present it to others.

KNOW GOD'S WORD.

God's Word renews your mind. Your thoughts won't always produce good decisions, but God's thoughts will. So you need to be thinking God's thoughts, seeing situations through God's eyes.

Psalm 119:7-14 sums it up well, especially verse 11: "I have hidden your word in my heart that I might not sin against you."

Knowing and obeying God's Word will help you make good decisions—starting with not sinning against God.

CHECK DECISIONS AGAINST YOUR MINISTRY'S MISSION STATEMENT.*

What's your ministry's mission statement? If a decision helps you flesh it out, it's probably a good decision. If a decision moves you away from your mission, it's probably a bad decision.

A clear ministry vision and clear goals make a lot of your decisions for you. Assuming you created them with the input and approval of your pastor and leadership, they're your marching orders.

But if you face a particularly tough decision, ask your pastor or supervisor for input. What decision will best serve your leader's purposes? You're here to serve your pastor, so actions you take need to line up with your pastor's goals.

Want to make it really easy for your pastor? Type up a brief e-mail outlining the issue, some options, and your recommendation. Then ask how your pastor wants it done.

MAKE DECISIONS THAT LINE UP WITH YOUR PRIORITIES.

If your top ministry priority is outreach, don't decide to spend your time designing costumes for an Easter pageant that only church people attend. If developing a mentoring program is something God wants you to do, don't decide to open a soup kitchen at this time.

---

*Need help creating a ministry mission statement? Check out *Children's Ministry That Works!* (Group Publishing, Inc., 2002) for a step-by-step guide, plus lots of other useful stuff.

It's not that soup kitchens and Easter pageants are bad things. They're good things. But they may not be the most important things you could be doing.

Clear priorities help you make good decisions.

SEEK THE COUNSEL OF WISE AND TRUSTED FRIENDS.

This is easier said than done. When we're facing a difficult decision, we often want to find people who'll nod sympathetically while we hold a "poor me" pity party. We don't really want counsel; we want an audience.

Ask for prayer support.

Proverbs 11:14 says, "For lack of guidance a nation falls, but many advisers make victory sure."

Great advice—but the point isn't to talk to as many people as possible. That'll tie you up forever, especially if you're just looking for sympathy.

When you ask for advice, don't limit yourself to people who'll sympathize with you. Rather, talk with people who might have answers. These people may or may not be your buddies. That's not the point. *They're people who have something to offer.*

And while you're at it, ask for prayer support. I've got people I talk with who almost never have answers, but they're prayer warriors. They pray for me as I wrestle through hard decisions.

Now is the time to identify wise people in your life who you can recruit as prayer warriors. Do it now, when there's no crisis to fix.

CHECK YOUR CHURCH'S POLICIES AND PROCEDURES.

Just the other day we got a new employee manual at Church on the Move. I've been at the church for years, but I still took the time to read it from cover to cover. I figured if I'm expected to enforce it, I'd better know what's in it.

When's the last time you read your church's policy manual? That's assuming you've got one, of course. If you don't, create one. How do things get done around your place? Who cuts the checks? What's the budget procedure? What's the procedure when you realize the budget that got approved isn't going to last past October?

You're probably not the first person to tackle whatever decision is facing you. How has it been handled in the past? The answer may already be in print.

If it's not written down, check to see how the youth department handles similar issues. Or the children's ministry in *another* church you respect.

And document how you solve a problem as you go through it. Why? Because you'll want to include that procedure in your next manual.

DETERMINE HOW MUCH CHANGE WILL BE REQUIRED.

Change isn't bad—but it can be uncomfortable. Before you make a decision that requires change, count the cost. What will it require of you? of others? of your organization?

If the change affects others, get their input. Not that you'll necessarily put the decision to a vote. If it's your decision to make, you be the one to make it. But take the people around and under you into consideration.

Ask yourself: Is the change best for your ministry or just for you? Leaders make decisions that benefit their mission and ministry, even if the decision is costly to individuals—including themselves. If you do initiate a change, beware of wet cement. The precedent you set may well outlive you. It can harden into a policy, and you'll be stuck with it…forever.

We have a deadline for camp registration at our church. We advertise, announce, and do everything but spell it out in skywriting. And every year, the day after the deadline, I get calls asking if I can squeeze one more child in…and then one more…and one more after that.

The answer is no.

So every year I have disappointed adults running around saying, "That Brother Jim is so mean. Did you know he wouldn't make an exception for me?"

That's right. Because the day I make an exception for one parent, I can toss the rules out the window. I've set a precedent I don't want to live with the rest of my life. And whoever follows me will appreciate my not setting it too.

RUN THE NUMBERS.

Not all decisions have to be based on numbers, but numbers are attached to most decisions. That's reality.

Your church budget is like your house budget—some weeks are better than others for making purchases. If the youth department just bought a new sound system, you may have to wait to replace that worn out carpeting down in the Sunday school classrooms.

Good stewardship demands you do homework on the numbers. It may be a good decision to buy top-of-the-line cribs for the nursery because they're safest and will outlast cheaper cribs. Fine—that's a financial decision you can defend. But woe to you if you make an expensive decision you can't explain when the questions come.

HAVE YOU PRAYED ABOUT IT?

You want to make a decision that honors God—so isn't it smart to ask him if he has anything in mind?

If at all possible, get the Lord's go-ahead *before* you make a decision. You'll sleep better.

12. Attracting Volunteers

Let's say your children's ministry is growing. New kids are coming every week, so classes are growing. There's more follow-up to do, more planning to do, and more kids to teach.

And when you look at your volunteers, you realize those precious folks are stretched thin. If you sardine just three more middle school boys into the classroom, their teacher will be in a hostage situation.

What will you do?

Most children's ministry leaders immediately go into volunteer seek mode. They ambush parents and beg for help. They call through the church directory. They convince the pastor to make a special announcement.

Their goal: *Get more staff.* But they may already have all the staff they need and just not know it. Or they may not be ready to handle more staff, no matter how badly they could use the help.

That's because when you pin them down, most ministry leaders aren't exactly sure which jobs need doing or how long those jobs will last. They aren't positive the resources needed to do those jobs are available or how volunteers will know whether they're being successful or not.

Man, there's *nothing* that scares away volunteer workers faster than your not being clear about what you need.

Why on God's green earth would anyone sign on to follow a leader who can't describe what he or she wants? It's like showing up to help a friend move and finding that the boxes aren't ready to carry onto the truck. You find the guy, who's fixing to get ready to go find boxes to start filling. He's not prepared. He's wasting your time. He's not ready to direct volunteers because he's still getting organized.

If you want to attract excellent volunteers, you've got to create a culture of excellence, an organization that's almost magnetic. Ministries like those not only attract great people, they hang onto great people.

I'm not going to list a couple dozen ways you can go out and recruit folks. There are already books that do a good job describing recruiting techniques.

What I'd like to do is back up a few steps and help you sort out the decisions you need to make *before* you start a big recruiting push.

- What sort of volunteers do you need—specifically?

- How can you recruit people who will not only help out now but help your ministry grow to the next level?

- What do you do if nobody ever seems willing to sign up? The problem may not be in your recruitment efforts—it may be in the culture of your church.

Like you, I value volunteer workers. We use about a thousand of them in our children's ministry. Without volunteers, the wheels would fall right off our programs. But I'll tell you: I'd rather have *no* volunteers than the *wrong* volunteers. If you want to get the right people in the right spots for the right reasons, here are ten bases you'll want to cover.

1. Determine *exactly* what needs doing.

Do yourself a favor: Make a list of where you need help in your children's ministry. What jobs do you need filled?

And don't just write down the bare minimum of what might work out if everything goes well and nobody calls in sick. Instead, ask yourself, "If getting excellent volunteers signed up were no problem, where and how would I use them—specifically?" Do you need a bilingual greeter? Someone to work with special-needs kids?

In my experience, children's leaders usually think they need more people than they really need.

The fact is that you don't just need "more volunteers." You have very specific needs for specifically gifted people. Not just any warm body will do.

Who do you really need that you don't have? Create your list. Now.

Then create a flowchart of how your ministry currently looks. Write in departments and names so you can see your ministry laid out in black and white.

Look carefully at your volunteers and where they're serving. Why? Because you may discover you've got too many leaders in one class and too few in another. Instead of rounding up more bodies, you can solve your worker shortage by moving a few teachers across the hall.

In my experience, children's leaders usually think they need more people than they really need. They can't tell you where they're fully staffed, understaffed, and perfectly staffed. When we try to keep everything straight in our heads, we miss obvious in-house solutions.

And speaking of obvious, here's something for you to remember: "You have not because you ask not."

Have you asked the Lord for the right people to come alongside and help you? Have you asked specific people to help? Have you asked for wisdom in planning for the future?

2. Identify the abilities you need in volunteers.

I think a lot of churches are like Frankenstein's monster: They have pieces in the wrong places.

You remember how that big guy lurched around with knobs sticking out of his neck? Whoever built him had dropped in a heart and sewed on a head, but there were definitely parts that weren't connected quite right.

We build a little bit of the monster into our ministries when we take people and plug them into the wrong places. We forget to ask what they want to do. What they're good at. What gifts, skills, and abilities they bring with them.

Paul used the human body as an example of how spiritual gifts work. Eyes and feet don't do the same thing. If you need a foot in your ministry, then putting an eye in that spot isn't going to work out for anyone. Not for the volunteer who'll feel frustrated, not for you, and not for the kids. We set people up for failure when we put them in the wrong spot.

I'm blessed in my church. The majority of the volunteers working in our children's ministry have been with us five years or more. We've had time to sort out who's an eyeball, who's an ear, and who's a foot. And we've also been able to create positions that accommodate different commitment levels.

Not that we always get it right the first time…

I got a call once from the parent of a two-year-old who told me that every time her child came to our Wednesday night services that child had nightmares.

Being the wise person I am, I knew right away that wasn't a good thing. I also knew that if I called the teacher of that class, I'd hear that nothing was wrong. So I kept my mouth shut and visited the class the next Wednesday.

It was wonderful at first. There was music playing, and the children looked so happy. I thought, "That mamma doesn't know what she's talking about. There's nothing here to give a child nightmares. Her kid's just demented."

Then the teacher gathered the children around him for the lesson. He plopped a sack next to him and after he said, "Tonight we're going to talk about the tongue." He reached into the sack—and pulled out a three-foot cow's tongue.

The teacher wasn't an evil guy, but his kids were all teenagers. He'd forgotten what it was like to be with two-year-olds. He didn't remember that you do *not* show a three-foot tongue to two-foot people or you will inspire major nightmares.

When the teacher unrolled that tongue and it flopped out at those children, there was crying and gnashing of teeth of biblical proportions in that room. And I discerned right quick that I'd identified the problem.

Was that teacher in the right place? No. Did he have a good heart? Yes. But he was most definitely a part out of place.

So I moved him to our fourth-, fifth-, and sixth-grade class, and my phone started ringing off the hook. Parents called up saying, "My son can't wait to come to church. When that teacher pulls things out of his sack, boy, that's exciting."

And it *was* exciting. Just a bit too exciting for two-year-olds. In this case, I was able to

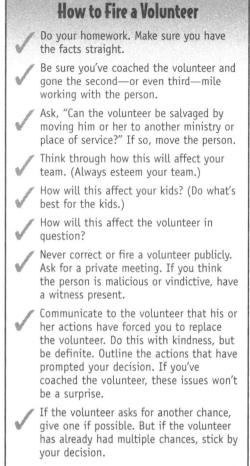

How to Fire a Volunteer

✓ Do your homework. Make sure you have the facts straight.

✓ Be sure you've coached the volunteer and gone the second—or even third—mile working with the person.

✓ Ask, "Can the volunteer be salvaged by moving him or her to another ministry or place of service?" If so, move the person.

✓ Think through how this will affect your team. (Always esteem your team.)

✓ How will this affect your kids? (Do what's best for the kids.)

✓ How will this affect the volunteer in question?

✓ Never correct or fire a volunteer publicly. Ask for a private meeting. If you think the person is malicious or vindictive, have a witness present.

✓ Communicate to the volunteer that his or her actions have forced you to replace the volunteer. Do this with kindness, but be definite. Outline the actions that have prompted your decision. If you've coached the volunteer, these issues won't be a surprise.

✓ If the volunteer asks for another chance, give one if possible. But if the volunteer has already had multiple chances, stick by your decision.

move the volunteer to a more suitable spot. But sometimes that's not possible. Sometimes you have to make the difficult decision to remove the volunteer. The checklist on this page will help.

3. Don't ask more than people are willing to give.

A chicken and a pig were walking down the street when the chicken saw an old, scruffy homeless guy sitting on the sidewalk up ahead.

The homeless man looked hungry, and the chicken felt sorry for him. So the chicken nudged the pig, pointed out the homeless man, and said, "We really ought to do something. Let's give that guy some breakfast."

The pig thought it over for a moment before answering.

"That's a nice little sacrifice for you," the pig grunted, "but for me it's total commitment."

The pig understood the situation clearly. A chicken can lay an egg and walk away to tell about it. But when a pig volunteers to add bacon, ham, and sausage as side dishes, it's an entirely different story. That's *total* commitment.

When we ask people to help out in children's ministry, people think we're asking them to lay down their lives, to quit everything else they're doing, and to live at the church. They think we want everything on the plate.

And maybe that's actually what you *do* want in a volunteer. If so, it's no wonder you don't have anyone around to help you.

It's great when you find lay-it-all-down pigs to join your team, but there's nothing wrong with recruiting a few chickens, too. Those people who are willing to do a job well and faithfully, but who won't give every Sunday, every Wednesday, and show up for all the church workdays, too.

There are people in my church who'll never consider teaching a class, but they'll pick up a hammer and build me anything I want. I've gone to folks and said, "I promise I'll never ask you to work in the Christian education department if you'll give me a hundred dollars every time I ask for it." They're business people who won't miss the money. They're happy to oblige.

I phoned one guy years ago and said, "I've got seven kids who need camp scholarships. Write me a check for seven hundred dollars." He pulled out his checkbook without a second's hesitation.

That's not a bad deal. Seven eggs with one phone call.

My point: You'll get more volunteers if you'll accept chickens as well as pigs. They'll lay eggs and be glad to do it.

4. Give people job descriptions.

Put jobs in writing. Now—before people show up. Here's why:

• You'll have a clear job description to hand a potential volunteer when God sends you that person. You and the volunteer will be talking about the same task. Your potential volunteer can make an informed decision.

• You'll avoid the temptation to create a job description based on a person rather than on the task you need done.

I once had a secretary who was just outstanding. Not only was she a real bulldog when it came to protecting my time, but she was a computer graphic whiz. In addition to helping me, she cranked out all our publications.

When she left, I had to make a decision: Was I looking for a secretary or a secretary/graphics specialist? Or did I need something altogether different? It had been wonderful having someone with her gifts and talents but was that what we needed to grow to the next level?

I outlined where we were and where I saw us heading, and it became clear that what we needed was a preschool director/secretary. I could hire out the graphics stuff easily enough, but our preschool was growing. I needed someone who could help with it for a while and eventually transition into running it.

If I'd just dusted off my first secretary's job description and advertised, I'd have replaced her. But I wouldn't have replaced her with someone who could do what we needed done during the next phase of our growth.

Start with describing the task as completely as you can, and *then* do your advertising. Bring people on board who are the right people to help you grow.

5. Focus on your current volunteers.

How to Write a Job Description for Volunteers

Here are the basics:

- ✓ What will the person in this role do?
- ✓ What skills, experience, and knowledge is needed for the person to be successful?
- ✓ When do you need the job done and for how long?
- ✓ With whom will the person work?
- ✓ To whom will the person report?
- ✓ What will the person get out of volunteering?

Here's one example:

Do you find fulfillment in helping others?

The parking lot ministry is seeking a patient, cheerful person to help visitors and church members move through the parking process on Sunday mornings. You'll smile at folks, pray for them as they arrive, and guide them to open parking spots.

You'll work with a team of kindhearted people and enjoy a cup of coffee and doughnut just before first service. You'll direct traffic for that service and then be finished for the day so you can attend second service to worship.

You'll serve rain or shine, so it helps if you enjoy being out in the weather.

You'll attend quarterly meetings (on Sunday morning) and be expected to participate for thirteen (13) weeks. Pastor Bob coordinates this ministry.

Maybe your next superstar helper is already recruited—but you haven't coached star-level performance out of that person yet. Look for potential in people and work with them. Don't always assume that your best helpers are still out there somewhere waiting to be lured in.

At my church, I regularly evaluate the people who report to me. That's helpful—but equally helpful is their evaluating themselves. People have a pretty good idea where they could use help. I ask the people who work for me to write down three areas where they want to see improvement in their skills, then together we tackle making improvements in those areas.

When we take the time to evaluate volunteers, we communicate that we expect a high level of performance. It's not enough in my children's ministry to just show up and read from the lesson book—kids deserve more than that. But if a volunteer does that for a few weeks and nobody says improvement is needed, what message is sent?

I don't wait until I've got a problem to find out if people are doing what they need to do or being where they need to be. I stop by and check up now and then. I watch. I listen. Then I'm able to provide better coaching, and there's another benefit: When I'm wandering around, everyone is doing their best.

Accountability helps recruit and retain volunteers because it communicates that you take what they're doing seriously. That what they're doing is important enough for you to make sure it's being done right. That matters, because nobody wants to sign up to do something that isn't important.

6. Raise the skill level of your staff and volunteers.

Here's where coaching comes in.

I think children's ministry leaders need to be excellent coaches. We can't be just good at it—we've got to be *great*.

A good coach knows the strengths and weaknesses of his or her players. The coach builds on what's there, shaping good habits and strong fundamentals. The coach thinks about individual players, always asking, "What could I do to sharpen this person's skills?"

And here's what's hard for coaches: They have to let their players go out and play the game. Maybe the football coach was an all-star quarterback in his past. That doesn't matter because *coaches don't play in the games.*

I guarantee no matter how many high school football games you sit through, you'll never see a frustrated high school coach slam down his clipboard and stomp onto the field so he can throw the touchdown pass himself. Throwing the pass isn't the coach's job—teaching someone *else* to throw the pass is his job.

Maybe the person who takes over your favorite job won't do it exactly as you do it. That's OK. So long as the pass gets thrown and someone catches it in the end zone, the team wins.

Good coaches delight in the success of their teams rather than their own successes. They catch team members doing something right and celebrate it. They don't need all the applause themselves—they're happy when they hear someone they trained getting the ovation.

If you're coaching well, you'll hear yourself asking these questions as you watch team members doing ministry: "What's that person doing well?" and "What can I do to help that person improve?"

If you're not asking those questions, there's no way your team will get to the next level. You'll be missing coaching opportunities.

7. Recruit constantly.

Want more volunteers? So does every other ministry in your church. Your biggest competition may not be the devil—or the youth group...or the ushers...or the bell choir...or the parking lot attendants. Your biggest competition is how people spend their free time, and people believing they have nothing to contribute.

Here's a tip: Ask the church office to run you a list of everybody in your church who's doing nothing. Then go find those people one at a time and personally invite them to come check out the children's ministry.

I approach people all the time and ask, "What are you doing in this church?"

"Nothing."

> **There are people in your congregation who need to be needed.**

"That's what I thought. Come with me."

I walk up to men of color in my church and say, "Listen—I need black male role models for little boys and girls who don't have men in their lives. Are you big enough to be that for them?"

I've never been turned down.

There are people in your congregation who need to be needed. Find them. When you connect with those folks, they'll be the most faithful workers you've ever seen.

The trick is to always be looking for people. When you find one who might work, reach in your back pocket and pull out your job descriptions. See if the person fits any of those. Determine if the person is spiritually and emotionally suited to work with kids. If it's a match, don't wait until the next recruitment drive to get that person plugged in; do it today. Now. This minute.

8. Use current volunteers to find more volunteers.

I don't know how to put this delicately, so I'll just say it: If you're the person in charge of finding volunteers, people in your church don't trust you. Even if they like and respect you, they're expecting you to sugarcoat things a bit when you're signing up workers. You've got a credibility problem.

But if it's your third-grade teacher who's says that teaching Sunday school is a blessing—*she* has credibility. Why should she lie? She's not the person carrying around the sign-up sheet on a clipboard.

So ask your team to recruit more staff. Your good leaders hang out with people like them. Ask leaders to tell their buddies about your ministry. It's your job to handle screening and training, but it's not always your job to find people.

9. Determine your church culture.

Let's say you're doing all the right things to get volunteers recruited and nothing is happening. No new workers. Not many returning workers. You're pretty much in this alone.

What's the message you should be hearing? That maybe at your church God doesn't want a children's ministry? Should you just up and quit?

Not yet.

Proverbs 22:6 says "Train a child in the way he should go, and when he is old he will not turn from it." That's Bible. It's true. And one place it's true is in how people live out their Christian lives.

I was raised in a time when people believed in the old adage, "Children should be seen and not heard." That *isn't* in the Bible, by the way, but in those days it might as well have been. The adults in my life were true believers when it came to those words. We had our share of fun, but there were definitely times I was supposed to sit up straight and be quiet.

And the times that this sit-up-straight-and-be-quiet rule was most severely enforced were those times I went to church. My job wasn't to worship or to listen or to take notes or to do anything. My job was to sit up straight and be quiet…or else.

So when I got older and started going to church, what do you think I naturally did? I sat up straight and stayed quiet. That's what I'd been trained to do as a child.

I had to get *untrained* before I could enter into worship. I had to get *untrained* before I could raise my hand to help out with children's ministry.

You've got people in your church who were raised to sit up straight and be quiet—I guarantee it. And you've got folks who were trained to think that the pastor does all the work. Their job is to come and drop money in the offering plate. And you've got people in your church who think of you as an entertainer. They tune in once a week and watch, but that's it.

If you want to have more volunteer workers, you've got some untraining to do. Ask yourself (and your pastor): Are people in our church trained to find places to serve? Are they trained to volunteer for things? Are they trained to see themselves as involved and invested?

If not, you're fighting an uphill battle when you're trying to recruit folks. Your culture doesn't support volunteering. Ask for your pastor's help in changing the culture.

10. Pray that the Lord sends workers.

A shortage of staff isn't anything new. Jesus himself described a harvest that was ready to pick, but there weren't enough workers to gather it in (Matthew 9:35-38). Your situation is probably the same. There are things you'd do if you had more staff. Needs you'd meet. Kids you'd reach.

If you believe more volunteers would help you accomplish what God wants accomplished through your ministry, ask God for more volunteers.

Just make sure you're ready to put them to use when they show up.

When workers sign up to serve in our children's ministry, they receive a thorough background check and are also expected to agree to the points listed on this form. We've found that clear expectations go a long way in avoiding problems later.

Use this form as an example for creating your own form.

Qualifications for all Church on the Move Helps Ministry Workers

Christians who are in places of responsibility in the church are required to be examples in faith, conduct, and business affairs.

One of the best ways to present Christ to the people of our community is by maintaining a high standard for workers. The following guidelines will be required of any person who works in any of the ministries at Church on the Move (COTM):

1. Must be in agreement with the tenets of faith of COTM.
2. Must be a member of COTM and have attended COTM for at least six months.
3. Must be able to make a minimum six-month commitment.
4. Must complete this application for helps ministry.
5. Must be loyal to the pastor and leaders of COTM.
6. Must be faithful to your assigned position.
7. Must live a separated Christian life.
8. Must attend all workers' meetings and workshops.
9. Must be faithful to attend regular church services.
10. Must give at least three (3) days notice if you know you will be absent.
11. Must be at your designated post thirty (30) minutes before starting time.
12. Must be neat in your appearance.
13. Must complete appropriate workers training course(s) required in your area of ministry.
14. Must have your home life in order.
15. Must give thirty (30) days notice when resigning your position.

I have read the above qualifications, and I am in full agreement with them. I pledge to keep them to the very best of my ability. I clearly understand that failure to keep any of the above requirements is grounds for dismissal.

Signature _____

Date _____

13. Staying Motivated

I've been exercising lately, and I'll tell you: It's easier to start an exercise program than to finish it. When you're pulling on running shoes and warming up, you imagine yourself out there pounding the pavement, waving to admiring people as you fly past them.

But when you're actually limping along, sucking wind, hoping you remembered to carry some identification so the paramedics know who to call—that's something different.

Starting out is easy, but it's tough to finish strong, especially when you're heading uphill.

So how do you stick with ministry when you hit those uphill times? When your budget is cut? When people complain? When you're taken for granted? It's at those uphill moments it's especially hard to keep making wise personal, family, and ministry management decisions.

Excellent leaders get discouraged just like everyone else—but they don't let themselves get stuck there. They move on.

I'd like to suggest ten ways you can move past discouragement.

1. Do what you do for the right reasons.

Colossians 3:23 tells us to do whatever we do with all of our heart for the Lord. That means you're not just working for a paycheck. You're not even just working for your pastor. You're working for the Lord.

I've already outlined some reasons leaders fail. But your goal isn't just to avoid failure—it's to be a success. And success in ministry is measured ultimately by hearing, "Well done, good and faithful servant!"

Are you making decisions to please God—or people?

Are you leading people the direction God wants to take them?

Are you in it for the right reasons?

If your motivations are anything other than pure, seek wise counsel and confess your shortcomings. Remember: Excellent, motivated, lasting leadership springs from a heart that's right with God.

2. Realize it's *your* job to stay motivated.

It's not your pastor's job to keep you motivated and growing. It's not your church's job. It's your job.

When I read the story of Moses, I see that Aaron and Hur encouraged and supported Moses. But ultimately, it was Moses who had to decide to keep his arms in the air.

Let me be clear: *It's not your pastor's job to keep you fired up.* I serve a pastor who spends time with me, and it's a blessing. But whether or not my pastor provides motivation and coaching, I still need to do what's on my to-do list to the best of my ability.

Take responsibility for staying enthusiastic about your ministry. Don't count on others to do that for you.

3. Stay in the Word of God.

Whenever you're shaken, what you've filled your life with is what will come out.

When problems arise in your ministry and shake you, if you're full of pride, then pride will pour out of you. If you're full of anger, that's what will spill out and splash on others.

But if you've been in the Word of God, faithful in spiritual disciplines, then that's what comes out.

Quiet time is one way to stay in God's Word, but let me add another one that lots of children's workers seem to overlook: *Go to church.* Not to lead but to rare back and worship God with your whole heart. Soak up God's love surrounded by other people doing the same thing.

I understand that if you're in children's ministry, Sunday is a workday for you. And if you're in a church with one service, I'm sorry—that puts you at a real disadvantage. But you still need to find a way to go to church frequently, no matter what.

Go for your own spiritual nourishment. Go to support your pastor. Go so people see you and know if they sign up to help with the kids' program, they can still go to church, too. Ask a strong volunteer to stand in your place and watch over the program while you worship. If they need you, they can get you.

4. Pray continually.

Things happen when you pray. In your situation. In your life. In other peoples' lives. And I believe those things *only* happen when you pray.

Pray and you'll have a more powerful, effective ministry. And when you see how God acts in and through you, that's tremendous motivation.

5. Choose to stay happy.

I'll tell you what: Life is just too short to not have fun.

> **I've yet to meet a thankful person who wasn't also happy.**

I don't know your situation or the challenges you're facing at church, home, or with your health. But Paul didn't know your situation either, and he had some great advice for you and me both: "Be joyful always; pray continually; give thanks in all circumstances, for this is God's will for you in Christ Jesus" (1 Thessalonians 5:17, 18).

I've yet to meet a thankful person who wasn't also happy.

Do this: Find people who make you laugh and hang around them. Cultivate those people and invest in them.

I make two pilgrimages a year to guitar shows, one in Dallas and one in Arlington. And I've made it a point to pull together a group of guitar-playing buddies who come with me. If you met these guys, you'd wonder how we could ever get along.

There's a dentist who's really conservative, and another guy who's a true good-ol'-boy redneck. Then there's the old hippie hairdresser. Another guy has played in bands all his life, and I don't even know *how* to describe him—except he's a great guitar player and a great guy. Then there's me: the children's pastor. What a crew.

I love those trips, and I enjoy them enormously. The dentist eggs on the redneck, we play jokes on each other, and we laugh until we cry. Being with those guys makes me happy.

Who makes you happy? Why aren't you seeing those people more?

6. Keep doing what God's called you to do.

Once you're in leadership, it's easy to get pulled into doing things that aren't really part of your calling. And when you quit doing what you're supposed to be doing, ministry can get discouraging fast.

In 1983 God spoke to me and told me to quit doing kids' crusades. I'd done dozens of them. I liked doing them. I was pretty good at it, too. God told me to quit handing out fish sandwiches and instead to teach people to fish. God told me he was calling me to teach teachers.

My function since that day has been to teach teachers. I've done it in addition to building a children's program in a great church, but it's never been a question in my mind if I should stop helping other leaders. God hasn't told me to quit doing it yet, so here I am, leading conferences, providing training tapes, and writing a book.

And man, it's motivating to do what God wants.

Where's your place in the body of Christ? What's your function? Are you there?

7. Lead people who'll follow.

The most discouraging, demotivating thing that ever happened to me in ministry has to be the time I called a worker meeting and three people showed up: me, my wife, and my mother-in-law. Man, that was a low point.

The church had just hired me as their first-ever children's pastor. And when I got on board, all the volunteers figured they could quit.

But I had a little group of sixth-graders who thought helping out was a big deal. So I worked with them, and we formed a puppet team. I'd have rather had a bunch of adult helpers, but none were willing. So I led the people willing to follow—a little group of sixth-graders.

Pretty soon they got their parents involved, and then the program took off. But if I'd sat around sulking, nothing would have happened.

You probably don't have all the volunteers you'd like to have. There are people you want who won't sign up. Forget about them. Lead people who'll follow.

8. Mentor someone else.

When you mentor someone else, you set an example. Someone else is depending on you to stay motivated so they can learn. I don't know about you, but I rise to that sort of challenge.

Who are you mentoring? What sort of example are you setting?

9. Be a self-starter.

You know what your function in the Body of Christ is, right? Let's say your role is to equip teachers to be effective in their classrooms. Then why not phone people in other churches with the same calling and ask what they can teach you? Search the Web to see what researchers know about it. Call up a professor in the college of education at the closest university and ask that Ph.D. what it takes to turn a college junior into an effective professional teacher.

Become a student of your job. Search for ways to get more information, better skills, a broader perspective. Keep learning.

There's a lot of motivation that comes with growing in your abilities and advancing your program.

And do this: *Get yourself evaluated.* If there's no evaluation procedure at your church, create one. Ask people above you to describe your strengths and weaknesses, and ask the workers who serve beneath you to do the same thing. These are people who see you in action—but what are they seeing? Invite them to tell you.

10. Refuse to quit.

Until I came to my current church, there was a pattern in my life: Every three to four years, I'd switched churches. I'd hit year three in a ministry setting and that's where I sort of lost momentum. So I left.

I was giving up too soon. I've watched ministry leaders, and I've observed that they really don't master their situations until the *fifth* year.

Here's the truth: Leaders who give up and move on seldom find greener grass at another church. They hit the same walls there, too, and usually in the same year.

So decide to stick where you are, asking God for grace to grow in your leadership. One thing for sure: It won't be boring.

14. How to Become a Next-Level Leader

6%
GRADE

A few years ago I was selected by Children's Ministry Magazine as one of ten "Pioneers of the Decade" in children's ministry. There was my picture in the magazine, smiling out at the readers.

It was an honor, but it got me thinking.

What was next for me? How could I take my ministry to the next level of service, effectiveness, and faithfulness? Would it ever be time to just coast?

For each of us, there's a *next level* of leadership. Whether we're just surviving or we're thriving and setting the world on fire, there's a next level for us. It's the level where we go from being *good* to being *excellent*.

What we've done at Church on the Move is pretty good. *Very* good. But there's always room for us to get better—to redefine the word *excellent*. As a leader, there's always room for me to sharpen my skills.

I've talked with dozens of excellent leaders. They're people whose ministries are growing, sometimes against all odds. They're influencing their communities. And they have a passion for their ministry and the people they're serving that is simply unstoppable.

I believe there are sixteen marks of a next-level leader who's growing rather than just maintaining. Most of these people aren't any smarter that you and me. They don't always have bigger budgets. They don't have superpowers.

What nudges these leaders from good to excellent has less to do with what they've got than with who they are. We'd do well to ask God to give us these sixteen characteristics in ever-greater measure.

I've touched on a few of these characteristics already, but let's look at them all together now—and see what we'll look like as next-level leaders.

1. Next-level leaders are driven people.

The idea of being "driven" has gotten a bad reputation. We think of driven people as living out-of-balance lives. We think they're out for glory and recognition. That's not at all what I mean.

Are you doing ministry but also watching the clock?

Driven leaders are motivated by a desire to excel in the work God has placed before them. They'll do whatever it takes to go from "good enough" to "excellent."

They'll study harder. Pray longer. Stretch themselves further. Work smarter. Master something they've never been able to do. They plug away until they have the skills to effectively lead others in ministry. They have enthusiasm for what they're doing.

Driven leaders may not work more hours than we do, but they're always thinking, always making connections that will improve their ministries. They're not motivated solely by a paycheck.

Here are questions only you can answer: Are you doing ministry but also watching the clock? Do you save your most productive, most creative hours for hobbies instead of your ministry? Are you giving your best?

2. Next-level leaders know where they are.

If you want to travel somewhere, you've got to have a destination. But before you get started, you need to know where you are. Otherwise, you don't know what direction will take you closer to your destination.

I knew a guy who went on a youth group ski trip to Colorado. The group members started out in Tulsa, and about the time they hit Kansas somebody pulled out a map to see how far they still had to go. Well, it was a lot further than they expected because they were headed *east*—and Colorado was *west*.

They discovered that their enthusiasm to reach Colorado didn't much matter because they were headed the wrong direction. They had their destination in mind, but they hadn't nailed down their starting point on the map.

Next-level leaders assess where they are. They have a realistic, no-nonsense understanding of precisely where they're sitting. And they have a plan to get to where they're headed, step by step.

Can you give a concise description of where you are in your ministry? What the next steps look like? How do you intend to get to your destination?

3. Next-level leaders know where they're going.

Excellent leaders can actually *see* their vision. They can *taste* it. They hear the sounds of children playing on a playground that hasn't yet been built. They smell the new seats of church buses that their checkbooks says they can't possibly afford.

They're determined to go where they believe God calls them, and the journey energizes them.

If a next-level leader believes God has called her to double the number of kids in Sunday school, she plans with that number in mind. She talks about that number at meetings and writes it on chalkboards. Her enthusiasm becomes contagious, and pretty soon she's surrounded by people who share her vision.

Listen to yourself at your next staff meeting. Do you sound as if you know where you're going? Do you hear yourself talking about little goals or big ones? Do you have a vision that gets people excited?

4. Next-level leaders have their personal lives in order.

Ready for a test? Ask your kids if they feel more important than your job. Ask your spouse. Ask your friends.

What did they say? Next-level leaders lead a balanced life that makes room for family and friends. Excellent leaders know that life is a marathon, not a sprint. Committees come and go; family is forever.

5. Next-level leaders keep changing their definition of excellence.

When they achieve a goal, next-level leaders don't stop and build a monument to their success. They reassess, set new goals, and move toward a new goal, a new definition of success.

A while back I got a baseball card in the mail, signed by a fellow who plays for the Marlins. He reminded me of the times we prayed together back in children's church when he was a little guy. He sent the card to let me know he'd reached his dream: He was playing in the big leagues.

Thousands of kids play little league, but very few make their little league all-star team. Of those young all-stars, few go on to play in high school. Few high school players play on a college team, and it's a very rare college player who's asked to play in the minor leagues. And of the hundreds of players competing on minor league teams, few make it to the majors.

I can guarantee this: A little leaguer's definition of baseball excellence is different from a high schooler's definition. What cuts it in college isn't good enough for the pros. For each level of play you want to move up, your definition needs to change.

6. Next-level leaders plan ahead. *Way* ahead.

The best time to plan for next year's VBS is the day after this year's VBS ends.

That's when your team is already assembled. That's when everyone remembers all the details, when you've got all the receipts and attendance charts in front of you. If you wait eight months to sit down and plan, you'll be lost.

Next-level leaders keep calendars that stretch out two, three, or four years. Not everything happens as they predict, but they still plan ahead. Excellence requires it.

How far ahead do you plan? What would change for you and your ministry if you doubled that time frame?

7. Next-level leaders delegate.

A next-level leader can look at a to-do list and know what's most important to do. And that excellent leader will know what *not* to do.

Forget that old idea that excellent leaders know exactly what's happening everywhere in their organizations. Really excellent leaders don't have a clue as to some of the details. But they know who does know. They've delegated some tasks and responsibilities to trustworthy people.

Look, if the devil wants to keep you from being successful in your ministry, he probably won't be able to trick you into taking drugs. And it's unlikely you'll suddenly leave your spouse or start embezzling the kids' mission offerings.

But if you can be convinced to spend all your time doing the wrong things, you'll be just as ineffective as if you were off doing some horrible sin. Next-level leaders don't do everything—they do the things only they can do. The rest they have other people do.

Wait a minute—I hear you saying, "Brother Jim, that's great for you. You've got hundreds of staff and volunteers to share the load. But I'm sitting here with a staff of just three: me, myself, and I. If I don't do things myself, they just won't get done."

Then don't do it. If you honestly can't take on another project, say so and let that task sit until you raise up someone alongside you to help. If you pull all-nighters and ignore your health and your family to get it done, then you'll never get any help. Why? Because you've proven you can do it yourself.

8. Next-level leaders bring order.

Next-level leaders bring order to a ministry by thinking through the steps it takes to reach goals, even goals that may be years away. Here's how I learned that lesson.

I wanted a worship band for our junior high ministry, but I couldn't find a drummer. Then I happened to look at the stage where the band would play, and I realized we didn't have any drums. Even if God had miraculously raised up a dozen drummers, I couldn't have used them. No drums.

We got a set of drums up there, and a drummer soon followed.

I was trying to go from "no band" straight to "complete band." I hadn't thought through the steps that would get us there. Next-level leaders do that sort of thinking, often on flowcharts. They can tell you the steps from point A to point Z.

Don't wait until you're a huge church to establish a culture of order. At Church on the Move we didn't. If you're a small church, act *now* to do the things that you'll be forced to do when you're a large church.

There was a time that our church had two buses. Here's how you got a bus for your ministry activity at our place: You'd walk through the church offices shouting, "Anybody using the bus next Friday?" If nobody hollered back, you assumed you'd reserved a bus.

I can't tell you how many times we got to the church and found the youth group, Sunday school, and senior citizens all standing in the parking lot, all expecting to use the same bus.

So our staff asked, "If we had one hundred buses, how would we operate?" I came up with a bus policy more than ten years ago and to this day we haven't changed it—though we now have sixty-five buses. We imposed order on a chaotic situation, and it's made everyone's life easier.

What are the organizational things that just bug you? that keep happening again and again? Those are probably items you could change for the better by creating policies and procedures that address them.

9. Next-level leaders train their people.

Let me be clear what I mean by *training*. I want to be specific because Christians tend to confuse *talking* with *training*.

At many churches, new Sunday school teachers are trained by getting a little lecture, handed a book, thrown in a classroom, and told to not come out until Jesus returns.

True teacher training is placing your new recruit alongside someone who knows what she's doing and letting your recruit watch awhile. Your new recruit gets hands-on experience and coaching, plus the chance to ask questions.

When the new recruit knows he can handle it, you give him some responsibility. Then, after he proves himself, you give him a bit more. And when he's mastered that, he gets even more. And on it goes.

Write this down in the margin: *There is no shortcut for training.* It takes what it takes. Excellent leaders understand that and invest in their people accordingly.

10. Next-level leaders connect with other leaders.

Some leaders become uncomfortable around strong leaders. I've seen very capable children's ministry leaders get tongue-tied and nervous around their senior pastors.

> Don't let someone's title or paycheck intimidate you; you're serving someone who owns the sheep on a thousand hills.

And for the life of me, I can't figure out why.

Listen: Other than your mother, there's nobody in the world who wants to see you succeed in your ministry to kids more than your senior pastor. One secret to your pastor's success is what you're doing over in the children's department. Your pastor is on your side, so why would you be nervous when your pastor strolls through the children's area to see what's up?

Mark my words: If you're uncomfortable dealing with strong leaders, you'll never be one yourself. Don't let someone's title or paycheck intimidate you; you're serving someone who owns the sheep on a thousand hills. If you're doing God's work, you have no reason to feel inferior to anyone.

11. Next-level leaders focus on meeting needs.

There's a difference between a program and a ministry. Don't create a program without first being able to describe what need it's designed to meet.

A while back our church decided to do something special for the college kids. All of us pastor-types sat down to discuss what we should do and eventually a radical idea popped up: Why didn't we just *ask* them? We had our ideas, but maybe they'd have some insight to offer too.

So we called in some college kids and asked them what kind of program would be meaningful to them and why. Our ideas weren't even close.

Now we base every program on meeting a need in the lives of our children, youth, adults, or families. And we don't guess—we ask. We ask kids, parents, and teachers.

What are the needs of children in your church and community? How do your programs address those needs? When was the last time you evaluated those needs? Next-level leaders meet the needs of the people they serve.

12. Next-level leaders manage people well.

If you're in ministry, you're in the people business. And to have a successful ministry, you absolutely must build and coach a strong team.

The place to begin managing people is to love them and want what's best for them. That attitude and commitment will help you now and when it's time to give your team suggestions and correction.

The fact is that if you don't care about me and you don't want what's best for me, why *should* I care what you think? You just want to be large and in charge. That's a far cry from being a beloved leader.

Let me just ask you this: Do you love your volunteers? Do you like them? If so, how do they know? How are you communicating your love?

13. Next-level leaders are problem solvers.

It's one thing to see the shortcomings in your ministry. It's another thing to fix them.

Here's something we do at Church on the Move: We work to eliminate excuses. When we plan a ministry program, we ask *upfront* what the excuses will be for not participating. Then we work to eliminate the reasons for those excuses before launching the program.

At one time, we found it hard to recruit bus captains—they're the people in charge of our bus routes. So we asked: "What excuses will we hear when we ask someone to serve in our bus ministry?" The answer was obvious.

Bus-ministry captains had to give up every Saturday, all year long, to call on kids on their routes. Would you do that? *I* sure wouldn't.

So I told my pastor I wanted to shorten the hours bus-ministry folks did visits. And now on holidays and four-day weekends when most kids aren't home anyway, we don't go out. That took us from asking a volunteer for fifty-two Saturdays down to thirty-six Saturdays. We eliminated an unrealistic expectation.

What excuses do you hear when people don't want to serve in your children's ministry? What can you do—without compromising the quality and effectiveness of your program—to eliminate those excuses *before* you ask for volunteers?

Check out Chapter 10 on becoming an effective problem solver for help with sharpening this skill.

14. Next-level leaders learn from other leaders.

Proverbs 27:17 says, "As iron sharpens iron, so one man sharpens another."

Your leadership won't grow from good to excellent if you sit alone in your study. You've got to go rub shoulders with people who are doing things right. Visit other churches and don't look at their shortcomings; look for their strengths.

Call up business leaders in your community, and ask them what they're doing to motivate their people, to read the culture, and to grow in their influence and market share. See what you can apply to your situation. And if the vice-president of marketing at Widget International gets intrigued with what you're up to, share the gospel with him so he understands.

Don't just stand on the sidelines watching other leaders. Ask them why they made the decisions they did and what they saw or heard in the situations that you missed. Squeeze every bit of coaching possible from time spent with excellent leaders.

And you don't even have to meet with every leader face to face who you admire. What are you reading these days?

I studied Colin Powell's book because if he can run the U.S. military, I figured he could help me organize our nursery. If Lee Iacocca could straighten out Chrysler, I thought he might have a few ideas for my preschool. I read Sam Walton's book because the guy who built the biggest retail organization in America might offer some suggestions that could help my elementary program grow. And I pondered the leadership principles of Abraham Lincoln because if he could put a war-torn country back together, he must have something to say that will help my youth group.

What's on your reading list this month? Anything that'll stretch your leadership? And what other leaders are you meeting and interviewing?

Remember: You can tell a lot about a leader by the company he or she keeps.

15. Next-level leaders don't try to do it alone.

Don't believe for a minute you can build a super-ministry all by yourself. It won't happen.

Winning coaches know that winning takes more than a strong first string. It takes a strong bench, too. If the same people always lead worship or preach in children's church, what happens when those people move on? You've got to be developing your next team, letting those second-stringers get some playing time.

And what happens if you move on? If God calls you to another church or calls you home? What happens to the ministry you've built then?

There is no success without a successor. If you love the kids and volunteer workers in your care, you'll have a plan in place to fill your shoes.

16. Next-level leaders have a shepherd's heart.

Some people are in leadership for all the wrong reasons. They enjoy the power and privileges. They like calling the shots. They feel bigger when they order others around.

But leadership in the church isn't about getting power. It's *never* been about getting power. In the kingdom of God, it's those willing to serve who please God.

If you're in ministry you'd better be there because you've got a shepherd's heart. You'll be successful only when you're determined to serve God and the people he's placed around you.

Next-level leaders are next-level servants.

How do people describe you: as a leader who's there to serve or to be served?

It's been my experience that next-level leaders—leaders who move from good to excellent—are characterized by the traits we've just discussed. I think these traits are so important that I've included a list of them on the next page. Post it where you'll see it often. Pray through it regularly.

The Next-Level Leader's Prayer

Lord, when I'm serving you and your people, "good enough" just isn't good enough. I want to lead and serve with excellence.

Today give me opportunities to grow in you. I want to become a leader who

- is driven and dedicated.
- knows where I'm going.
- knows where I am.
- has my personal life in order.
- keeps changing my definition of excellence.
- plans ahead—*way* ahead.
- delegates.
- brings order.
- trains my people.
- connects with other leaders.
- focuses on meeting needs.
- manages people well.
- is a problem solver.
- learns from other leaders.
- doesn't try to do it alone.
- has a shepherd's heart.

Lord, thanks for the privilege of serving. In Jesus' name, amen.

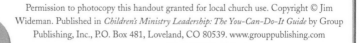

15. Lessons From a Forgiven Father

I asked someone in children's ministry the other day if she was full time at her church.

What a silly question!

Of course, she's full time at her church. They may pay her for full time, part time, or not give her a nickel, but she's still working full time. I don't know anyone in children's ministry who's *not* full time. It's just that sort of job.

I've already mentioned that when I started in children's ministry I left a secular job and gave up my spot in a band for less money than I was making in the band alone. I didn't just take a pay *cut,* I took a pay *amputation.*

But because my wife and I knew it was the Lord's will, I went full time at the church. I was so excited that I'd be able to work full time with boys and girls. What a tremendous opportunity.

I soon discovered that I'd had more time for kid contact when I was a volunteer. As a staff person, I now had days for counseling and hospital visitations. The shut-in ministry and a ton of administrative stuff landed on my plate too.

If I wanted to take care of all that *and* have kid contact, I'd be working more than forty hours a week, that's for sure. And you're probably in the same boat. Children's ministry always takes more time than you expect.

Excellent children's ministry usually takes even more time than that.

And there's the conflict: How can you be an excellent children's ministry leader and an excellent spouse and an excellent parent at the same time? When we look at our ministry to-do lists it sometimes feels as if we're expected to sacrifice our families on the altar of ministry, doesn't it?

Well, don't you do it. You can't afford to do it.

There's another way.

Ministry Starts at Home

I believe that from the get-go we've got to first and foremost minister to and care for our families.

This isn't just my opinion either. I believe it's what God's Word teaches. After all, God established the home before he established the church. And 1 Timothy 3:5 says, "If anyone does not know how to manage his own family, how can he take care of God's church?

I know a lot of people in ministry who have this backward. They take care of the church first and then worry about home. They think their church work is more important than their home.

Not true. If you're a parent, your primary children's ministry is with your own children. If you win every kid in your city for Jesus, but you don't have time for your own children, I believe you're a failure. If that seems harsh, I'm sorry—but I think it's true. You've got a God-given responsibility to tend first to your own children and then to other kids.

Read Deuteronomy 6:6-7. It's the parents' responsibility to train up their children in the things of the Lord. It's not something that can be delegated to a children's pastor. And if you *are* the children's pastor, it's not something you can hand off to your spouse or to the children's program at your church.

Listen—we all know horror stories about ministry leaders whose kids can't stand going to church and who reject the things of God. One reason is that often these kids learned early on that for Daddy or Mommy, church was more important than them.

I have friends in ministry whose children aren't living for God. These are children old enough to be making their own lifestyle decisions, and unfortunately they're choosing to not honor God.

My friends would give anything—anything—to turn those children around, but they can't. It's up to their children now.

These parents did what they could. They're still doing what they can. But I'm sure there's not a day that goes by without their wondering if there's something else they could have done. That's not a discussion you want to be having with yourself in a few years, so focus on your children now. Teach them. Disciple them. Encourage them. Have fun with them!

And give them a home where they know that they're more important than your career. Not by your words alone but also by your deeds.

I can't fill the role of Daddy for every child in Tulsa. God has called me to be the father of two wonderful girls, and that's it. I can be an example to other kids, but they can find other examples. I can be a leader in the lives of other kids, but there are other leaders.

My two girls can never find another Daddy. That's where I can't be replaced and don't want to be replaced—so I guard that precious opportunity.

And if you don't have kids, don't think you're off the hook. Are you married? Then your first priority needs to be your home, not the children's ministry program.

It's my wish that Julie never regrets for a day that she married me. That she knows every day that I love her, cherish her, and thank God for her. I want our marriage to be strong and fulfilling for both of us.

Spending all my time at the church or every night of the week at a meeting won't get me what I want or give Julie what she deserves. It won't create a home that honors God and is a great place to live.

God established my home. I'm not being a poor leader if I protect and nurture it for his glory—and our joy.

Moses Messed Up—*Big* Time

Figuring out how to balance being a ministry leader and a family leader isn't a new problem. And neither is failing to do it right.

In Exodus 18:2-6 we see that Moses was having some trouble at home. Big trouble. So big that he and his family had separated. Moses had sent away his wife, Zipporah, and his two sons. They went to live with Moses' father-in-law, Jethro.

You cannot build your ministry on the ashes of your family.

But Jethro was a smart guy. He didn't let them stay long. He brought them back to Moses and then stuck around for a few days to see if he could figure out the problem.

Jethro discovered Moses was wearing himself out in ministry. Moses was wearing out the people of Israel, too. And if Jethro was the father I think he was, when he had a heart-to-heart talk with Moses, I'm sure he also threw in, "And this isn't real good for my daughter and grandkids either."

Now there was nothing wrong with Moses wanting to do a good job as a leader. But Moses had crossed a critical line. He'd sacrificed his family for his ministry.

Listen—you cannot build your ministry on the ashes of your family. You can't say, "I'm doing this for God, and he'll just have to take care of my spouse and kids."

Your family *must* be your first priority. And not just in the future, after you've made it through the Easter pageant, or you've got your second service up and running, or you get a bigger church.

Your family has to come first *now*. You won't be able to take your spouse on a vacation next year and somehow make up for treating your spouse as a second-class project this year.

I'll be honest: When I first started in ministry, I had a hard time balancing ministry and family life. Like Moses, I wasn't organized enough at church to keep my job under control. That put me in a hole both at work *and* at home.

I've straightened that out, asked forgiveness, and it has been absolutely worth the effort.

If you want to be an effective leader, find a way to put your family first. Letting your family take a back seat to your ministry is a surefire way to not only ruin your home life but undermine your effectiveness as a leader.

Maybe you've got this all under control. Fine—but test it. Ask everyone in your family: Have you ever felt that you were less important than my church work? If so, when? And how did that make you feel?

Ask your kids and your spouse to be honest—and mean it.

And even if you hear that you're always available, always attentive, and always wonderful, find ways to improve.

I believe that it's never too late to fall in love with your family and for them to fall in love with you. You may have high school kids who've checked out of family life, but if they're still in your house, you can start doing things right. You can reach out to them. You can confess that you had your priorities out of line, then make changes that will influence them and their behavior.

Here are ten keys to building a strong family in a ministry household. I know they work—because they've worked for me.

1. Have a vision for your family.

We set visions for our ministries—why not our families?

What's your vision for how your family will look and behave? for how you'll serve God together? for how each member of your family will develop his or her individual gifts for service? What do your children want to accomplish?

If you don't set goals for your family, you're aiming at nothing in particular, and I can guarantee you'll hit it. Everyone will get older, maybe your kids will get married and have kids, and sooner or later everyone will die. Is that all you're after?

My two children are as different as night and day. They don't even *look* like sisters. The younger one is six inches taller than the older one. They have different colors of hair, different temperaments, and completely different goals.

God made my daughters unique people, and he put them in our family for a reason. I want to help them both develop their gifts and find a way to use those gifts to serve God. That's not the job of their Christian education director—that's the job of their parents.

What's the vision for your family? for each member of your family?

2. Desire to be close.

Psalm 37:4 says, "Delight yourself in the Lord and he will give you the desires of your heart."

I have a retired next-door neighbor who's a handy guy. Now that he's fixed up everything at his house, he's hanging around my house, fixing up things there. I come home and the gate's been re-hung. He calls me and says that since he's picking up fertilizer for his yard, he'll pick it up for mine, too. This is not a bad deal.

He's gotten a close-up look at my family because I've got a *lot* of things that need fixing. The other day he said something to Julie that just broke our hearts.

"Your family is so close," he said. "Watching your family makes me wish I had wanted a close family when my kids were little." His granddaughter comes to visit occasionally, and he hardly ever sees his son. My neighbor shook his head and said, "I really made some mistakes. I just didn't desire a close family. There were other things I wanted instead."

Don't get me wrong: I don't think my neighbor is a bad man. He was trying to provide for his kids during the years they were under his roof. But that didn't communicate love to his kids, and he didn't have a desire to connect—and that's a decision that cost him.

Believe me, if you're going to have a family that survives the ministry, you'll need a family that desires to be close.

And I believe with all my heart that part of what will earn you a "Well done, my good and faithful servant" will be how you led at home, not just at church.

3. Schedule time to be with your family.

Is your family important enough to you to rate a spot in your schedule? Mine is, and they know it. They can open my appointment book and see their names right there in ink.

One thing my wife and I have started doing is walking together in the morning. Besides my needing the exercise, there's the added bonus of entertaining the neighbors as they see the cute, thin woman walking her fat husband around. I think they look forward to that.

And for us there's the bonus of having time together. We get to talk—*without* the kids—and that's a treat. Whenever a few days have gone by and our schedules have kept us from walking, Julie will say, "I really miss our walks."

That's my cue. I know I need to go walking. Not just for the exercise, but because she needs time with me. And you know what? I need that time too.

Communicate your schedule to your spouse. My wife has been in ministry with me for more than twenty years, and she knows when the busy times will be as well as I know them. She knows when I'm going to miss a week or two of dinners because I'm at church.

But I still check in with her to make sure she knows. I still call if I'll miss a dinner. And I expect her to do the same with me.

I'm a big believer in our doing things together. My wife once said that she thought we needed a hobby we could do together. I figured she'd suggest golf or something like that.

But she said, "I'd like to start shooting."

Shooting?

"With a *pistol*," she said.

So for Mother's Day, I got my little ninety-pound wife a pistol. Being a good redneck, I already had four or five, so I knew right where to go to get her one.

And then, every so often, we'd go out shooting. Sometimes we'd take the girls. We called those outings "lead-fests." There the Wideman family would be, out in the middle of nowhere, shooting up a storm.

I'm not suggesting that target-shooting is necessarily the activity you should do together as a couple or as a family. But find something to do that you enjoy together, and do it.

I'll tell you this, though: If you're thinking of dating my daughters, you might want to note that their Daddy and Mommy have pistols. And they know how to use them. For that matter, my *daughters* are pretty good shots too.

Consider yourself warned, gentlemen.

4. Go on dates.

When you schedule time to be with your family, you're honoring and serving your family. And when you schedule dates with your wife or husband, you're just being smart.

> **When you venture into your family members' worlds, you communicate that you care.**

If I intend to keep my wife, I have to keep doing what I did to win her heart in the first place. I've got to keep calling her. I have to go places with her. I have to send cards and flowers. I have to spend money on her. That's what I did when we were dating. Why stop now?

When I go out with my wife, I dress up as best I can. That's because I want to show her that I'm honored to be with her. It's a matter of respect.

And may I suggest another way to spend time with your family? Tag along when someone in your family is going someplace.

At our house Julie does most of the grocery shopping. I don't particularly care to go shopping, but it's an awfully cheap date. Especially if I don't put extra stuff in the cart.

I used to hate the mall, but my daughters have memorized the place. And when I go with them, we have a great time. They put on a fashion show, and I've learned how to make the right sort of appreciative noises, even if I'm mostly looking around to see how the department store lit up the shoe displays. Man, I can always use good lighting ideas in my puppet shows!

Here's my point: When you venture into your family members' worlds, you communicate that you care. With a little effort, you can redeem "chore time" and turn it into "communication time." Almost anytime can be a date if you approach it with the right attitude.

One final piece of advice: Don't forget getaways! Agree on the frequency that you and your spouse will go be together alone for a long weekend. Even if you're busy. *Especially* if you're busy.

The church members will understand. So will your pastor.

5. Disciple your children.

Matthew 28:19 is pretty clear: "Therefore go and make disciples of all nations, baptizing them in the name of the Father and of the Son and of the Holy Spirit."

Somewhere in one of those nations are your children. It's your job to disciple them. And that, my friend, takes time.

If you want to see your children grow in the Lord, you've got to make a commitment to be together as a family and also to regularly spend time one-on-one with each of your children.

You earn the right to disciple people when they believe you love them.

A few weeks ago, I took my youngest daughter, Whitney, out for Chinese food. The rest of the family doesn't like it, but we had a great time talking together as we chowed down on chow mein.

My other daughter, Yancy, and I caught a Steven Curtis Chapman concert together a few days later. We like to take binoculars to concerts and try to figure out what styles and models of guitars the musicians are using. People who sit next to us think we're nuts, but we don't care. We have a good time.

No way could I switch activities with my girls. They have unique likes and dislikes, and I know that because I've entered into their worlds. I know what brand clothing they each like. I know that now and then, because they like to dress up, I'm going to get dragged off to the Dove Awards or a musical.

If you want to disciple children, you've got to consistently be in their lives, looking for teachable moments, watching for chances to share God's Word.

A confession: I've never been much of a family-devotion guy. I'm not big on setting aside a half-hour every week to get religious with my family. Man, I think our *entire* life together needs to be a devotion! I talk about the Word and how it fits into our daily life as daily life unfolds. Are devotions good? Sure—but so is being always on the alert for opportunities to discuss life as it happens.

I'm big on praying with my children, and I hope you are, too. Raising a child requires prayer, so you might as well include your child in the process.

Are you spending time with each member of your family? Do you know your spouse's favorite flower and movie? each child's favorite activities and radio station? You earn the right to disciple people when they believe you love them. Give your family members all the evidence in the world that you're crazy about them—each of them.

6. Train your children.

Your kids need your example. It's one thing to tell them what's right and another thing to show them. That's when lessons get memorable.

Do this: Make a list of all the things you want your children to be when they grow up. All the character traits and all the personality traits. Then get busy becoming those things yourself so you can be a model.

You want them to be honest? Let them catch you being honest with your taxes. You want them to be patient? Be patient as you're driving.

Find other adults who demonstrate the attributes you want to see in your children, and have your kids spend time with those mentors. Surround your children with God-honoring people, and let your kids soak it all up.

> **Surround your children with God-honoring people, and let your kids soak it all up.**

Encourage your kids to ask questions, too. Especially the hard questions.

I knew there was going to come a day my daughters would look at me and ask, "Dad, did you and Mom have sex before you were married?"

I was so thankful that I knew Jesus when I was dating Julie. We purposed in our hearts that we'd stay pure until we were married, so I've been able to look Yancy and Whitney in the eye and say, "Nope—but it's been great fun since our wedding."

My kids know me. They know I took drugs back in the '70s. They've asked me hard questions, and I've answered them.

And I've discovered this: Training never stops. There are character issues, career development, and if you're lucky, discussions about people they're dating.

Encourage your kids. Catch them doing right things. And be sure to believe in your children, especially in their dreams.

I've taken some flak about how I've gone about helping one of my daughters pursue her dream of being a rock-and-roller.

Now, if she wanted to be a painter, I'd take her to some art shows. She'd see some good stuff, some bad stuff, and learn to know the difference. And I'd want to expose her to the best art I could so she could see the masters.

Well, when you want to be a rock-and-roller, that principle still applies. You've got to go see the masters at work—so I had my wife take my daughter to a Rolling Stones concert.

You can imagine how some of the people at the church responded to *that*. Maybe you've got some questions too.

But can you think of a better example of longevity in rock-and-roll? Those guys have been around *forever*. I keep expecting a Stones' tour to be sponsored by Depend underwear and the AARP. The Stones have been packing out auditoriums for decades, and anyone who wants to make a life as a rock-and-roll musician can learn something by watching their showmanship and staging.

There's a real strength in your being next to your children when they

smell marijuana for the first time at a concert. They're with you—there's a safety net under them as they get exposed to something that can hurt them. My rock-and-roll daughter won't even consider playing in clubs because I've taken her to clubs to hear bands. She's smelled the cigarette smoke and seen how people get when they're drinking, and she wants no part of it.

Are you entering into the worlds of your children and your spouse? Are you there to provide training when it's required?

7. Guard your time off.

Even God took a day off. And you're trying to keep running week after week without a day off? Who do you think you are?

The fact is that you need rest. And your family needs to know that if you're with them, *you're with them*. If you interrupt a game or a video four times to take phone calls, what kind of message do you think that sends?

I let my family help me figure out what to do on my days off. It just makes sense: I want to be with them, so I might as well do things they enjoy. That policy has opened up lots of new experiences for me. For instance, I know more about designer makeup than I *ever* thought I'd know. And you'd be amazed at what a guy who looks like me can know about ballet.

8. Look for ministry tasks to do with your family.

Do what you can to include your family in your church work, too. When my children were young, I asked them to come with me when I had to run errands for the church. One of my children helped me pick out 190,000 pieces of candy for a Hallelujah Night event. She thought that was *way* cool.

What are you doing that your children could help you do?

It's a fine line, though: You *force* the ministry on your family. You don't want to penalize your children for having a parent who's a children's ministry leader.

Here's what I mean: I got a call from a church worker who was getting flak about putting her own kids on stage during a children's ministry show.

I asked her, "If they weren't your kids, would they still be in the show? Are they gifted and talented in that way?"

"Absolutely," she said.

"Then don't worry about it," I told her. "Go ahead and use them."

Listen: If your kid is the right kid to sing the solo in the Christmas program, let him sing the solo. If your child has the best costume in the contest you hold on Hallelujah Night at your church, give her the trophy. If people don't like it, they can lump it. Those folks can just grow up.

I don't want my children to be penalized because Daddy was called to the ministry. I want my children to cherish the call of God and recognize it as a benefit in life—not something that becomes a burden.

9. Don't bring home problems from the office.

Let your home be an oasis, a sanctuary. When you come through the door and see your kids, don't lose those first few moments of reconnecting because you're dragging home stress and anger.

My goal is to not let something that happens at work affect my attitude toward my children. Is that your goal too?

Whether your kids greet you at the door with a big smile and a "Daddy's home!" or they're hunkered down in the basement listening to CDs and hardly know you're alive, make contact. That's easier to do if you're not complaining about the work your pastor expects from you or about the call you got from a youth volunteer.

Make sure your spouse and children know that coming home to them is the high point of your day. And that you want to enter into their worlds, not drag them into yours.

I'm not suggesting you lie about how your day went. Don't pretend everything's fine if it isn't. But what will your fourteen-year-old son do about the way the church board voted on that new computer you wanted for the ministry? Does griping to your son help your cause—or teach him to resent the church?

And here's a tip that was incredibly helpful for me: If you must work at home, do it in a way that lets your family know whether it's OK to interrupt you or not.

When I'm tackling a job that doesn't require complete and total concentration, I do it in the family room. My kids wander in and out, ask me questions, tell me jokes, tell me about their day—and it's fine. I don't get through the work quickly, but that's OK. I'm staying connected to my family.

Now, if I don't want to be interrupted, I go hide out for the minimum time necessary in the computer room. That's the signal that Dad shouldn't be interrupted until later.

I spend as little time as possible in the computer room.

And consider this radical concept: If your kids are little, don't work until your kids are in bed. They'll drift off to sleep smiling because you cuddled them, tucked them in, and prayed with them. And you won't stay up all that much later.

10. Admit it when you make mistakes.

If you're going to have a good family life, one of the best things you can do is be transparent.

There are times when I have to ask my family for forgiveness. I remember some years ago God showed me that I wasn't spending enough time with my family. I wasn't there for them in the way God desired—and, when I slowed down and thought about it, in the way *I* desired.

I sat them down, asked their forgiveness, and then repented. I changed my priorities and adjusted my schedule. I showed them I was sincere.

God wants you to have an excellent ministry—and an excellent home life. It's not that you've got to choose one or the other.

Wise leaders choose both.

16. Lessons I've Learned the Hard Way

DO NOT ENTER

I was leading a ministry conference in Springfield, Missouri, and we had a few minutes before things got started. Rather than sit around doing nothing, I asked if anyone had questions.

A guy raised his hand and said, "Tell us about some of the mistakes you've made."

Now I knew that I'd messed up now and then, but until I started talking about it, I had no idea I'd done so many silly things.

I'm so glad there weren't video cameras when I started in children's ministry. Boy, if you could see some of the stupid stuff I did, you'd want your money back for this book.

I've written about the "Great Egg Drop" (see Chapter 8). That certainly didn't go as planned. I never did *that* again.

And there was the time I took a little fellow to camp who happened to be blind. I knew he was blind, but I didn't know that he'd had his eyes removed and replaced with glass eyes. Before he got into the lake, he took his glass eyes out. *That* got the attention of the other children.

I could have gone on all day telling stories on myself, and you know what? That probably would have been fine. People like to hear about mistakes we've made, and not just so they can get a giggle at our expense.

We can learn from the mistakes of others. When you tell me what you did that fell down, or blew up, or fizzled and fell flat, I can tuck that away as a lesson learned. I won't try it myself, and you've spared me a painful experience.

If you're growing in ministry, you'll find yourself in the same place I am: doing lots of things for the first time. I've never before been in a situation where I'm pastoring thousands of kids. There are lots of times my workers look at me when we hit a new challenge and say, "Brother Jim, what are we going to do?"

And I have to say, "I haven't got a clue."

That's the thing about being a pioneer: You see a lot of unfamiliar territory. When you add a new after-school program in your church, you're being a pioneer, and that means there's a lot of potential for making a mistake—but also for reaching new kids. When you put new playground equipment in your side yard, you might make a mistake—but you can also bless your kids.

Successful leaders make mistakes— and they learn from those mistakes.

Anything you do that you've never done before can be a place you make a mistake...but what's the alternative? To always do what you've always done? That's fine, but there's a consequence: You'll always get what you've always gotten.

When you grow, you make mistakes, but mistakes aren't the worst thing that can happen to you. Far worse is to do nothing. And even worse than that is to make a mistake and learn nothing from it.

Anybody who's growing makes mistakes. Have you ever watched a child learn to walk? Mercy, it's a good thing children's little behinds are padded because they spend a lot of time landing on that padding. Very few children just stand up, dust themselves off, and take off walking.

The Wright brothers tried to get an airplane into the air for four years and hundreds of attempts before they figured out how to get the engineering right. They kept learning from their mistakes and making adjustments.

Abraham Lincoln ran for—and lost—elections for the Illinois State Legislature and the U.S. Senate (twice!) before getting himself elected president. He learned something from each effort to get himself ready for the next try.

Successful leaders make mistakes—and they learn from those mistakes. It's not the mistakes that stop us; it's what we do with those mistakes.

There are times I wish I could go back to churches where I've served and do things differently. That I wish I could plan activities differently or say something I didn't say.

Except I can't go back—and you can't either. You can only choose to go forward. And you can thank God that he's a God of second chances.

Here's some of what I've learned from my mistakes. These are things I wish I'd known when I started in ministry. I hope you'll benefit from reading these and that you'll be able to learn from my experiences.

Say no to a know-it-all attitude.

God's Word has a lot to say to people who think they already know it all.

In Proverbs 9:9, we read, "Instruct a wise man and he will be wiser still; teach a righteous man and he will add to his learning."

The key to being productive is to keep learning. You can learn something every day—if you want to. Make it your prayer to always be on a quest to learn what God has for you to learn. I'll guarantee that you don't already know it all now.

If you're busy trying to convince others that you already know it all, you won't be teachable. You also won't be making any friends. Nobody comes alongside arrogant people when they trip and fall.

Build a team. Don't be a one-man show.

Let me tell you what happened when I left a church in Alabama to come to Church on the Move.

I'd trained and prepared leaders to capably direct the midweek programs, the VBS, the puppet team, and the Sunday school. But I'd always enjoyed leading the children's worship time, so I'd reserved that job for my family and me.

After I'd been gone awhile, I asked some folks from that church how things were going. They told me they'd had their best VBS ever. The Sunday school was growing, and the midweek programs booming.

But then I asked about the children's worship services. And that's when someone said, "I've got to be honest with you, Brother Jim. Thanks to you, we have *lousy* praise and worship time."

Ouch.

That had been the one area where I'd been selfish and kept it for myself. I hadn't duplicated myself by training other people, so when I left, there was no one ready to take over. In that area of ministry, there was no fruit remaining after I headed off to Oklahoma.

That's when I decided that no matter how much I enjoy doing some things myself, I will always prepare a successor. I'll create teams with a depth of skills and experience. I'll leave fruit that remains after I'm gone.

You owe it to the people in your church to do the same thing. There's no success without a successor, and when you prepare people and release them into ministry, you release yourself, too.

Think God's way.

Philippians 4:8 says "Finally, brothers, whatever is true, whatever is noble, whatever is right, whatever is pure, whatever is lovely, whatever is admirable—if anything is excellent or praiseworthy—think about such things."

I think all children's workers ought to know this verse—right down to their bones. Why? Because the key to a good attitude is how you think.

Don't think negatively about people. Remember the good things about your workers, your pastor, your church, and the kids you serve. Focus on the positive.

And I'm not talking about sugar-coating anything. I know you don't have perfect people on your team. And you know what? They don't have a perfect leader. I'm not asking you to ignore the weaknesses of people. I'm just asking you to love those people. To see them as God sees them.

It'll revolutionize your life—and your ministry.

And do this for me: Think in steps. I know you usually hear, "Think big! Dream big! We serve a big God!"

We *do* serve a big God, but he's a God of order too. And when he created the universe, he did it one step at a time. So why do you think you can jump across all the steps from here to something huge? Think small, not big. Think of how you can make one corner of your ministry excellent, and then move on to the next corner. And then the next. When you get back to the first corner you fixed, you'll have learned enough to improve it even more. Then start your route over, improving things as you go.

Consider other people.

When I was single and didn't have children, I used to plan things at times that made no sense for parents and families. Then I'd wonder why people didn't show up. What unspiritual people!

They weren't unspiritual. They just had a children's pastor who didn't consider them when he set the calendar.

Who are you serving? Do you think like those people? Do you think like the people you're discipling and training for ministry? If you don't, you'll never be effective.

And think like a visitor, too. You know where all the classrooms are in your building. You know where to find the bathrooms and the light switches. Your visitors don't—so you'd better find a way to tell them with signs and a greeter or two.

Learn from others.

I used to think that I had to come up with all the great ideas and solutions myself. I used to spend days re-inventing the wheel.

Now when I run into a challenge, I pick up the phone and call someone who's dealt with that problem before. People are happy to spare you the hard knocks they experienced if you'll ask for advice and be teachable.

Study people who are successful. Look for models of ministry that work in situations like yours, and then borrow ideas that are helpful—but make those ideas your own. You can't expect a program that works wonderfully in Oklahoma to fly in New York without some major modifications. Be willing to do that work.

Commit to the long haul.

Early in the ministry, I was quick to give up. Things would get tough, so I'd pack up and leave.

I was talking with my pastor the other day about the fruit of staying put in ministry. It's so neat to see kids I had in children's church now fulfilling the call of God in their lives as adults. I'm glad I didn't give up and leave when things got frustrating, or I'd never have seen that.

fear is faith in reverse— and perfect love casts out fear. You don't have to be afraid of failure. Just serve, and let God be your provider.

I wish I'd been committed to the long haul earlier in my ministry.

How do you do that? How do you stick year after year?

Don't let *leaving* be part of your vocabulary. My wife and I agreed when we got married that we wouldn't let divorce be an option— ever. We wouldn't even use the word. We'd live by the Word of God, stay true to each other, and work through whatever came along—together.

If you're going to make a relationship with a church, work long term; it takes that same sort of commitment. You've got to be willing to put your dreams on the back burner and serve others, trusting that God will take care of you and your dreams in his own time.

A few days ago I pulled into a gas station and was filling up the tank. A guy walked out of the station and said to me, "Brother Jim, I want you to know you don't have to pay for your gas. I've paid for it. I want to say thanks for what you're doing for our kids, and this is a small way to say that."

You know what that was for me? It was way more than a free tank of gas. It was a reminder that God will care for me and my family. I don't have to be afraid of failure, and I don't have to be afraid of losing my job. I can just stick here and serve God, my pastor, and the kids in our ministry.

Fear is faith in reverse—and perfect love casts out fear. You don't have to be afraid of failure. Just serve, and let God be your provider.

Don't try to do everything overnight.

Have realistic expectations for yourself. You can't do everything. You can't do things instantly. Creating a solid, long-lasting ministry takes time.

Listen: Rome wasn't built in a day, and there were a *whole lot* of Romans working on the place. Don't be surprised if it takes you awhile to build something too.

Don't take part in power plays.

When I was young in ministry, I tried to get my way all the time. That approach to life doesn't work when you're a child, and it doesn't work when you're a grown-up.

As children, we throw fits and demand things. We're loud and angry. As adults we get all concerned and work the angles, pretending that we're really just concerned about our ministries.

Don't pout and don't threaten. I once worked for a pastor who deserves an award for putting up with me. I'd ask for something, and when he didn't jump to do what I wanted, I'd threaten to leave.

One day he'd had about all he could take of me. "All right," he said, "go ahead and leave."

Well, I didn't want to leave—not really. I just wanted my way. It was the best thing he could have said to me. After he called my bluff, I never threatened anyone that way again.

Think about the well-being of others. Of your ministry. Of your church. Be a team player. Esteem the team.

Be willing to lose a battle to win a war.

We just have to defend ourselves, don't we? We just have to be right. We'll fight even silly battles to make sure people know that we're right about something.

Sometimes it's better to keep your mouth shut and not defend yourself so you don't get sucked into stupid arguments. Besides, it's God's job to defend your reputation.

I once worked on a church staff where the pastor wanted to build a certain sort of building. We'd done some research and had a proposal, but there was an architect on our board—a nice guy with good intentions—who wanted a different sort of building. He'd drawn up plans to show us what he recommended.

The pastor and I got together, and we studied the architect's drawings. We found weaknesses, some things he had in the wrong place and things he'd forgotten to take into consideration. So I did my homework, boy, and at the board meeting I not only presented our idea, but I poked serious holes in the architect's work. I made him look truly dumb.

The pastor and I got what we wanted—our proposal was accepted. But when I got home I couldn't celebrate. I'd gotten my way, but I'd done it at the expense of a godly man who was just trying to help.

I felt guilty and convicted, and I deserved it.

I should never have tried to make someone else look bad, and that's exactly what I'd done. I should never have demanded on getting my way, whatever the cost.

I wish I'd learned those lessons earlier.

You can't attract workers sharper than you are.

I used to ask my wife, "Why do I have so many hippies and bikers working for me?" They were fine people, but I wanted to get at least a few bankers or teachers signed up to teach a class.

Then I looked in the mirror. I looked like Easy Rider. I cut over ten inches off my hair, and it was *amazing* the sort of people who started volunteering.

Look, if you want to have long hair, have long hair. I'm not going to tell you that everyone has to look or act the same. But I will tell you this: If you want a sharp business owner to volunteer, you've got to develop the skills and look of someone that business owner can respect.

As leader, *you'll* set the limit on what sort of people your ministry can attract. It's important how you look and act—and what level of leadership skills you've mastered.

Put your family second only to God.

If I'd known early in my ministry what I know now, I'd not have planned family vacations around ministry functions. I wouldn't have used all my time off visiting my parents and extended family.

Build memories with your immediate family. Don't ever let your spouse and children suffer because you're in ministry.

For the first six or seven years I had children, I was still concerned about becoming a success. I worked all the cotton-pickin' time. And then it hit me: The biggest success I could possibly have was to establish a family that loved God with all its heart. And that wasn't going to happen with Daddy taking care of everyone but the people who lived at home.

Guard your time off. Take your time off. Guard your nights. Enter into the lives of your spouse and children in intentional, caring ways.

How you carry yourself reflects your respect level.

Dress appropriately. Represent your pastor well. Don't be goofy and silly.

Listen, just because you're a children's pastor doesn't mean you have to walk around with a balloon sculpture around your head every Sunday. Just because you're a youth pastor doesn't mean you need to go out and get holes drilled in your body so you can wear piercings. Don't worry about being cool.

There's *nothing* that will turn off a group of kids quicker than someone going through a midlife crisis. Kids already know they're cooler than you, so don't try to compete. If you love those kids and you're glad to see them, they'll love you back. It's really that simple.

Don't build loyalties to yourself.

I wish I'd known this earlier. I used to get close to people, and then they'd leave the church. Why? Because I talked to them about things I didn't need to be talking about. I ran down things that I should never have shared.

It's true everybody needs a best friend—but that person doesn't have to be from your church. Never confide too much in volunteers or church people. And by all means never talk negatively about people in leadership above you.

Be your pastor's biggest fan. Make your pastor look good. Remember: You're on staff as an invited guest and as a servant. If I could change anything about how I lived out my early ministry life, I'd never build loyalties to myself—I'd build them to my pastor.

I've taken down every picture of myself at our church, but there's a picture of our pastor in every classroom. That's because I want kids to know that *he's* their pastor and I'm his representative. If they can't see him in me, I'm a poor representative.

It's never too late to learn.

I've had people come up to me at a conference and say, "Boy, I wish I'd heard some of these things twenty years ago." Well, me too. The fact is that twenty years ago they'd have had to find someone else to teach it because I didn't know it twenty years ago.

It's never too late to change. It's never too late to start doing ministry differently. And it's never too late to learn from the mistakes of others—including my mistakes.

God-honoring leaders care more about hearing, "Well done, good and faithful servant" than about getting a pay raise. More about being authentic than being applauded. More about servanthood than selfishness.

And always and ever, leaders wake each day knowing God has an adventure out there in front of them. That adventure may take them around the world or around the corner to buy balloons for this Sunday's children's sermon—but they're headed somewhere. God is leading them somewhere.

Ready for adventure?

Take the next step today.

Lead!

You can do it!